KING OF TRAVELERS

JESUS' LOST YEARS IN INDIA

EDWARD T. MARTIN

2nd Edition Published by:
YELLOW HAT PUBLISHING
A DIVISION OF YELLOW HAT PRODUCTIONS, INC.
5190 NEIL RD., SUITE #430
RENO, NEVADA 89502
WWW.JESUS-IN-INDIA-THE-MOVIE.COM

King of Travelers
Jesus' Lost Years in India

First Edition Copyright © 1999 by Edward T. Martin
Second Edition Copyright © 2008 by Edward T. Martin and Yellow Hat Productions, Inc.

All rights reserved.

No part of this book may be reproduced or utilized in any form or by any means, electronic or mechanical, including photocopying, recording or by any information storage and retrieval system,
without permission in writing from the Publisher.

Inquiries regarding this book and other Edward T. Martin books about Jesus in India should be addressed to info@jesus-in-india-the-movie.com or to:

YELLOW HAT PUBLISHING
5190 Neil Road, Suite 430, Reno, Nevada 89502

PUBLISHED BY YELLOW HAT PUBLISHING IN ASSOCIATION WITH THE ORIGINAL PUBLISHER, JONAH PUBLISHING COMPANY

First Edition
First Printing September 1999
Second Printing November 1999

Second Edition
First Printing June 2008
Second Printing December 2009

Edited by Paul Davids
Cover design by Jordan Duvall
Jesus image for cover design adapted from artwork by Alexander Tomlinson
and used with permission
Book design by Paul Davids based on design of first edition by Terry Sherrell
Photographs by Edward T. Martin
Map of return to India reprinted with permission from Dr. Paul C. Pappas
Poster of "Jesus in India" the Movie © 2008 by Yellow Hat Productions, Inc.

ISBN Information for this Second Edition:

ISBN-13   9780981924434

ISBN-10   0981924433

I dedicate this book to the adventurous and open-minded explorers and researchers who pioneered the inquiry into the subject of Jesus in India.

Among those explorers:
Nicolas Notovitch
Swami Abhedananda
Nicholas Roerich
Aziz Kashmiri
Mrs. Clarence Gasque
Madame Elisabeth Caspari
and many more

and to Paul Davids
who edited this edition of this book
and who had the courage and foresight to
undertake producing and directing the film
inspired by this book and by my research:
"JESUS IN INDIA"

"Climb up on the backpack of the writer, peek over his shoulder, and enjoy this awesome, challenging and delightful journey."

> R. Leo Sprinkle, Ph.D.
> Counseling Psychologist
> Laramie, Wyoming

"An exciting, exhilarating journey which expands our consciousness and understanding of the real Jesus and his true meaning for us today. This encompasses an enlightened perspective – an eye-opener and soul-opener! Spellbinding, thought-provoking… "

> Barbara Lamb, M.S.
> Author / Psychotherapist
> Claremont, California

"Edward T. Martin's research propelled my interest in this extraordinary topic that led to my making the film **"Jesus in India.**"

> Paul Davids
> Producer / Director
> Los Angeles, California

MANY THANKS to my wonderful parents, Tommie and Dorothy Martin; my memories of them are evergreen. Thanks to Gladys Darnell and Lila Foster for their help and kindness. Thanks to Paul and Sandy Huffington for encouragement and words of wisdom and good cheer when I needed them. Thank you to Rev. Alan Stanley and Rev. Ramiro Serna for wise spiritual guidance. Thanks to Rita Abrego and Elmo Guernsey for being friends and kindred spirits. Thank you to Barbara Lamb, Helen Billings, and George Kruse for friendship, spiritual wisdom and encouragement.

A special thanks to Dr. Leo Sprinkle of Laramie, Wyoming for taking time to read my manuscript and then writing the marvelous Foreword for this book. Special thanks also to Ed Reaves of San Antonio, Texas for his excellent skills as an attorney and for his support and encouragement.

Thanks to Stephen Bright for his marvelous work with photographs and to Alexander Tomlinson for creating the image of Jesus seated in the Indian lotus posture, which was adapted by Jordan Duvall for the preparation of her wonderful cover art for this second edition. Thanks also to David Sutton and Fortean Times magazine, first publisher of Alexander Tomlinson's art concept. At Morgan Printing in Austin, Texas, I want to thank Terry Sherrell for the wonderful work she did with typesetting and editing the first edition, which was initially printed in 1999. Thanks also to Mark Hillis for his sage and helpful advice. Thanks to Sky Skylar for her helpfulness and good cheer. And a big thanks to Paul Davids for his editorial contributions to this second edition and to Yellow Hat Publishing for making this publication possible.

Thanks to Larry Katkin of Fairbanks, Alaska, for telling me years ago that I would write this book. He was right!

Thanks to Greg Ferland of Colorado for his wise insights, support, and encouragement.

Thanks also to my many friends in India and elsewhere throughout Central Asia, without whose help this book could not have been produced.

Lastly, my thanks to the one whose name means "the arrow of death against the untruth."

Foreword

Have you got your ticket? These words often were used by a friend of mine, now deceased, to invite someone to a new challenge, whether it be a physical journey, an intellectual exploration, or a leap of faith.

If my friend were alive, he thoroughly would enjoy reading **King of Travelers: Jesus' Lost Years in India** by Edward T. Martin. He would appreciate the rigors of walking through rugged and isolated territories; the tolerance for dealing with everyday people who are experiencing everyday problems in living, and the faith of a true Christian who seeks the truth as well as the enlightenment of Jesus the Christ.

Ed is a person of many dimensions: tanned and compact, he is a rugged outdoorsman; intelligent and curious, he relishes an historical mystery; generous and helpful to those around him, he seeks to renew the faith of others in the power of love as taught by Jesus.

Edward T. Martin has provided us with a ticket: a marvelous opportunity for a new journey, a new insight, and a new faith in the miraculous life of Jesus, Saint Issa (also often spelled as Saint Isa), Jmmanuel, et al.

For persons who read the book and experience the message, there will be a profound gratitude for the author, Edward T. Martin, and for his courage and commitment to truth. And those who read the book will certainly want to see the film it inspired: **"Jesus in India"** (www.jesus-in-india-the-movie.com) and will want also to read Edward T. Martin's companion book: **Jesus in India: King of Wisdom – The Making of the Film & New Findings on Jesus' Lost Years in India**.

Ed is among several writers, e.g., James W. Deardorff, Ph.D., who have analyzed the problems of the New Testament and the evidence that Jesus spent a significant part of his life in India. The legends and written documents are quite consistent, whether the source be Buddhist, Hindu, Christian or Muslim writers.

Some persons may pick up the book but decide not to embark on the journey. They may fear the loss of a cherished image of Christ as a distant God. Or they may fear that the "gospel" (good news) is based upon self-responsibility and self-education.

A dogmatic Christian may refuse to look at the evidence, rather than exploring the evidence for the historical Jesus having sought out and preached to the peoples of Asia and India. I hope this won't be the case, because I believe that same Christian could benefit from noting the influence that continued in so many communities from the teachings and healings of Jesus.

Which is better: a frozen image of shame and suffering? Or a living and loving image of a traveler who continued his ministry of love and commitment to all of humanity? If you choose to delve into this evidence and explore it, you will understand that it is with good cause that Jesus is known among many in the Muslim world as "Saint Issa, King of Travelers."

You Have Your Ticket!

So climb aboard the backpack of the writer peek over his shoulder, and prepare yourself for visions of places and faces, climes and cultures, and the mystery of Jesus' lost years.

In my view, Ed Martin is an excellent teacher and writer – and a true Christian: He seeks to live like Jesus / Issa / Jmmanuel, as he walks and talks in many communities with many people, whether they are rich or poor, powerful or hapless, ignorant or enlightened. He shared his coin, courage and compassion with all those who are on the same path: *The Journey of the Soul.*

Enjoy the Journey!

R. Leo Sprinkle, Ph.D.

*Counseling Psychologist
(and Professor Emeritus,
Counseling Services,
University of Wyoming)
Author of* **Soul Samples**

"All great ideas begin as heresies."
— George Bernard Shaw

"All over Central Asia, in Kashmir, Ladakh and Tibet and even farther North, there is still a strong belief that Jesus or Issa traveled about there."
— Jawaharlal Nehru,
Glimpses of World History

"A Traveler! By my faith, you have great reason to be sad; I fear you have sold your own lands to see other men's; then, to have seen much and to have nothing, is to have rich eyes and poor hands."
—William Shakespeare,
As You Like It

"I should not talk so much about myself if there were anybody else whom I knew as well. Unfortunately, I am confined to this theme by the narrowness of my experiences."
—Henry David Thoreau,
A Week on the Concord and Merrimac Rivers

PREFACE

"And there are also many other things which Jesus did, the which, if they should be written every one, I suppose that even the world itself could not contain the books that should be written."

— The Gospel of John 21:25

    This is admittedly an unusual book, but it is a work that I hope will advance the search for possible solutions to one of the greatest Biblical mysteries. Part of the focus is on the many missing years in the life of Jesus Christ. The missing years, unaccounted for in the New Testament except for one sentence in Luke, are from the age of twelve until the year he began his ministry, said in the New Testament to be about the age of thirty. I have reasons to believe that many of those years were spent in India, Nepal, Tibet, Iran and possibly other countries of the Middle East and Asia as well.

    Hopefully, my readers will accompany me on this quest to attempt to separate legend and myth from historical events that actually occurred but have been buried – in some cases buried by lack of mention by Christian orthodoxy, which has had its own interests, priorities and directions in defining Christian history and belief in the past two thousand years… and in other cases, quite literally <u>buried</u> in the sands of Egypt and Israel.

    These were the so-called "apocryphal" texts – written works about Jesus that were more or less contemporaneous with the canonical books of the New Testament but were excluded from the process of assembling and creating the Bible. These texts were hidden in caves or buried in sand to prevent their destruction by those who disagreed with their contents. It turns out that these apocryphal works include writings in the Far East, specifically Tibet, Ladakh and Kashmir.

It's a daunting task to sift for the "excluded" facts of actual history, and one for which some critical information and documents are still lacking. The answers may never be established to the satisfaction of everyone, the way many other historical issues are finally resolved. But this book is more than conjecture, based on at least one document seen and translated numerous times by reputable people but not available to researchers today. The reasons why it is unavailable are not entirely clear, but the search continues. This document, called *The Life of Saint Issa, the Best of the Sons of Men* (Saint Issa referring to Jesus), must have existed or must still exist, based on the testimony to date. How old it is has not been determined.

If as many have conjectured, it does date to the years soon after the crucifixion (as it purports) then it is momentous. And it would be right in line with what Hindu philosopher, sage, author and teacher Paramahansa Yogananda claimed throughout his lifetime – that the Three Wise Men of the New Testament were Indian rishis or advanced souls who paid homage to Jesus at his birth, and that Jesus later repaid the visit, so to speak, by traveling east to spend much of his youth in the ancient land of India.

The Nicolas Notovitch book, *The Unknown Life of Jesus Christ*, based on the ancient document *The Life of Saint Issa*, has been the object of much unjust (in my opinion) debunking. The longest statement about this subject by Yogananda is to be found in the rather recent publication by his organization, Self-Realization Fellowship. It is a compendium of Yogananda's writings related to Christianity, called *The Second Coming of Christ: The Resurrection of the Christ Within You*, a beautifully presented two-volume set published by the Self-Realization Fellowship.

Still another document on this subject, known as *The Talmud of Jmmanuel*, is claimed to be the document Biblical scholars have long referred to as the "Q" document upon which the four canonical Gospels of Matthew, Mark, Luke and John were based. This has not been proven, of course.

And the existence of that document is challenged by many, as its existence rests on the testimony of one man. Although the story of the discovery and destruction of that "purportedly ancient document" raises a myriad of questions and doubts, nevertheless, at least one scholar (Dr. James Deardorff) has come to the conclusion that the document must have been genuine. Dr. Deardoff concludes that it correctly answers many mysteries about the life of the man we know of as Jesus but who may have been known as Jmmanuel (with a "J"). The Bible occasionally hints at this in saying that the saviour would be known as Emmanuel.

A second focus of this book is about the intriguing but disturbing (for most Christians) possibility that Jesus did not actually perish on the cross, but that he was in a state of near-death and recovered, fled from the Roman Empire and continued the Messiah's mission of seeking reunification of the "Lost Tribes of Israel," some of which were scattered in the Far East, including in Kashmir. By this possibility, his post-crucifixion appearances to his disciples were real, historical events, but not necessarily supernatural events. This line of inquiry has him later returning to India, marrying and living a long life – eventually being buried there in an ancient tomb that is in the heart of a Muslim district in Srinagar.

At first, I completely rejected even the possibility that such a thing could have happened, because I did not want to believe it, despite the evidence I was finding. It seemed impossible that Christianity could have developed in a way that made it completely immune to acknowledging any of these "facts," if in fact such things historically did occur.

It was more comfortable, back then, for me to cling to what I had been taught as a child, even if I sensed it might not have been fact. But as I grew and explored, that gradually began to change.

A third focus of this book is personal narrative about my own spiritual journey and some very unusual but very real experiences that profoundly influenced my world-view.

In telling this narrative, I have included personal, direct experiences, which although not precisely connected to the Jesus in India subject, will hopefully be very intriguing nonetheless -- and certainly contributed to what I would like to think of as my expanded or open-minded point of view about things that many in society regard with a narrow view. This, in turn, makes some of the conjecture or speculation in this Biblical search possible.

I have saved the more controversial of those stories for the latter part of this book.

My travels have been many and my adventures (some bordering on the paranormal, perhaps, and others positively life-threatening) have been unique. Not many people are either "obsessed" enough or unconventional enough in their outlooks and manner to seek out the same experiences which I have undergone. In some cases, I have gone through many hardships willingly, always for a higher purpose, beginning with arduous mountain climbing excursions throughout the world. When contemporaries of mine were placing emphasis on material advancement, I was looking for other mountain peaks to climb.

Let's return for now to the subject of the many 'lost' years in the life of young Jesus. Why is it that our vast Western civilization, which is overwhelmingly Christian, expresses so little curiosity about those missing eighteen years? Obviously, Jesus lived through those years; he was somewhere. But where was he and what was he doing? Why do our traditional New Testament Gospels hide those years from us? What is being covered up and why?

Was Jesus just fiddling around in his father's carpentry shop, happily humming away, making tables and chairs? Why did he waste so much time, piddling around, one might ask? What was he waiting for? Why didn't he start his ministry much sooner?

For that matter, there is no real evidence at all that Jesus became a carpenter. There is only an assumption of that, because in those days sons often took the same profession as their fathers. But not always.

Many people overlook a very important historical point: Jewish boys and girls of that time were normally expected to get married at the age of twelve or thirteen years. That was a powerful social and cultural part of expected, proper behavior. The expectation was even stronger for a very intelligent, good-looking, healthy boy from a decent family.

Certainly, the fathers of eligible, attractive girls would be approaching Joseph and Mary to discuss the situation: "Which girl will Jesus marry and how soon? When will you decide?" Certainly, the pressure would be building. For a boy intending to become a rabbi, a spiritual teacher, the expectation of marriage, if anything, would be even stronger. Any boy who stubbornly refused marriage would perhaps be considered indecent, crazy, physically unable, or just weird. It certainly would have put a burden and disadvantage upon any such boy in that place and time.

However, when Jesus began his ministry and was apparently single, he had no such disadvantage of negative public opinion (at least, until he declared in a synagogue that the scriptures were now fulfilled in the sight of those present, bringing on the wrath of the worshippers in the temple).

What could explain the fact that his status as a single man of about thirty was not in itself a basis for rejection? Perhaps the most plausible explanation is that he was physically absent for many years. One acceptable reason for not marrying was that of traveling extensively, for example, for the purpose of studying in foreign lands. One could hardly expect such a person to put a spouse through the many hardships of long travels. Such a person could be expected to marry later.

Let us also not forget that Jesus had brothers and sisters. The Gospels speak about those siblings in Matthew 13: 55,56. If Jesus decided to leave home secretly at, let's say, the age of thirteen, he could have written a farewell letter to his parents, explaining that he was going away to study and would return after some years. Then he could slip away at night, walk some distance and join a camel caravan going eastward to India.

In those times, a strong boy of thirteen would be considered a man, and a caravan leader could always use a helpful, trustworthy young man. Mary and Joseph would be upset, yes, but they had other sons and daughters to think about. The parents knew that their son had a lot of maturity and good judgment for his years, and besides, they would see him in the future. Recently, I heard a lady minister at a Unity Church say jokingly that she wished her son had gone away at thirteen and reappeared later. Life would have been much easier, she said.

Another possibility is that young Jesus may have had a sponsor, a wealthy patron. Levi Dowling, a Union Army Civil War Chaplain, put that possibility forward in his beautiful book, **The Aquarian Gospel of Jesus the Christ**. In that book, Prince Ravanna from the eastern India state of Orissa was visiting Jerusalem and became the sponsor of Jesus.

Considering the long history of the written word and record-keeping in India, Pakistan, Nepal and Tibet, it is possible that more written details of the youth and later life of Jesus may be uncovered in the future. More surprises may lie ahead.

"Where there is smoke, there is fire" goes the old saying, and there is a tremendous amount of smoke regarding the subject of Jesus in India!

Not only may there be undiscovered ancient historical documents, but the recent advances in DNA testing and forensic medicine may open up unimagined possibilities for exploring the truth.

One additional reason I have written this book is because I want to make myself available to help and encourage people in their spiritual search. I want to help people of all ages, but especially young adults, people who are beginning their search.

One analogy I have heard is that of the word "triage."

The triage concept was developed by French battlefield surgeons and it goes like this: of all those wounded, about one-third would die anyway, another third were slightly hurt and would live anyway. The middle third of the triage were between life and death and could go either way. That group was where the major attention was placed.

I'm certainly not a surgeon, but what I mean by this analogy is that many people are between light and darkness in their spiritual search and could go either way.

Perhaps I can encourage some people in their search for the truth to look a little deeper and not be so quick simply to accept what they were taught at a young age.

As the statement is made in the **"X-Files":** "The Truth is out there." The *Truth*, the queen of all our dreams, is seldom the simplisitic explanation of reality we are offered as children. However, *Truth* is glistening, pouring in like beams of bright sunlight into a forest of darkness. May the truth vanquish the darkness.

Personally, I think that finding the truth about the subject of Jesus in India will transform our thinking and the way of life of many Christians, changing us all for the better by adding to our insight, wisdom and spiritual maturity.

I hope you enjoy my search as much as I have enjoyed undertaking it.

                              Edward T. Martin
                              Tucson, Arizona
                              Revised July, 2008

"And Jesus increased in wisdom and stature
and in favor with God and man." Luke 2:52

That's all the Bible has to say about Jesus from Ages 12 to 30.
Where was Jesus during those years?

A PAUL DAVIDS FILM

Jesus in India

Table of Contents

1. A Very Strange Bottle of Beer 23
2. Journey to the Vale of Kashmir: Heaven on Earth 41
3. A Meeting with the Author of *Christ in Kashmir* 55
4. Journey to Dharamsala, India: Home of Tibetan Refugees 66
5. At the Taj Mahal and Beyond: A Dream in White Marble 74
6. Kathmandu in the Kingdom of Nepal 82
7. Traditions About the Teenage Years of Jesus 109
8. Traditions of Jesus in Lhasa, Kashmir and Tibet 120
9. Unusual Events 128
10. I Learn About the *Talmud of Jmmanuel* 161
11. How Do You Like Your Jesus? 175
12. Some Closing Thoughts 184
13. Bibliography 190
About the Author and the Motion Picture 196

KING OF TRAVELERS

JESUS' LOST YEARS IN INDIA

"We are going again, this time to Central Asia, where, if anywhere upon earth, wisdom is to be found, and we anticipate that our journey will be a long one."

— H. Rider Haggard, *She*

A Camp of Nomads, Koh-i-Baba Mountains, Central Afghanistan

1. A Very Strange Bottle of Beer

> *Whenever a human being sets out to find the real truth about something, he must first arm himself with great courage, because he may not find what he is expecting.*
> —Jiddu Khrishnamurti

With a roar, the Ariana Afghan Airlines jet burst downwards through the dense cloud cover and began the descent toward Kabul, Afghanistan. The jagged, snow-capped peaks of the Hindu Kush, the "Hindu Killer" mountains, the western extension of the Himalayas, sprawled beneath us.

A strange-looking array of mud buildings, turbaned men with rifles slung on their shoulders and a caravan of two-humped, Bactrian camels loomed below. I looked around at my friends as we all stared out the windows of the aircraft. We all had an eerie feeling. It was as if we were about to arrive on a strange, alien planet. In a sense, we were.

I was a young Peace Corps volunteer about to be stationed in the central Asian country of Afghanistan. After three months of Persian language and cross-cultural training, our group of about 35 Americans would be sworn in as volunteers and given work assignments.

I had volunteered for the Peace Corps because I wanted to do some form of national service for my country, the United States of America. In World War Two, my father, Thomas F. Martin, had gallantly volunteered to serve in the Army Air Force. He died suddenly from a heart attack when I was nineteen.

Another reason I was in the Peace Corps was because I had the strong desire to visit India. Yes, I had grown up in a small town in Texas. Every summer we had gone on family vacation trips to different parts of the United States. By the time I finished high school I had seen many parts of the U.S.A. But India? I can't explain it, but since I was a child, I had wanted to go to India. I was keenly interested in spirituality and other religions, such as Hinduism and Buddhism. I wanted to explore things firsthand.

A third reason for being in the Peace Corps was pure red-blooded, rip-snorting, hell-raising adventure!

I wanted to see the world! Especially the Third World, the developing countries of Africa, Asia, and South America.

I wanted to have my own firsthand, direct knowledge of the world. I wanted to check things out personally, and see if the things I had been taught were really true.

I wanted to think independently, outside of the box, and to draw my own conclusions.

And I wanted the fun and thrill and adventure of traveling to exotic lands and experiencing the diversity, beauty, and wonders of this planet.

Street Scene, Kabul, Afghanistan (note woman on right wearing a full veil)

Part of that firsthand knowledge also, would be my own inquiry about human nature. For example: why do human beings on planet Earth love to fight so much? I'm not talking about self-defense, which is necessary. I'm talking about excessively hot-tempered, over-aggressive, war-loving behavior. Somehow, to me, something seemed out-of-whack, just wrong. Are humans supposed to be like that?

Sawdust used as winter heating fuel

Another thing I had puzzled about is how rapidly humans get old. I had even at times seen high school students with gray hairs. Or people in their twenties or thirties beginning to look like old people. Why did the Old Testament in the Bible tell of people routinely living hundreds of years? I was always on a search for explanations for both of those puzzles.

In any event, philosophy and aspects of wonder were always on my mind, even as I embarked on the trip to Afghanistan.

In Aghanistan, our group of about thirty-five volunteers were taken first to a dormitory-type building in the Shari-Nau (New City) section of Kabul.

It was December that year of 1973, and the weather was cold and icy, with occasional snowfalls. Our rooms were heated with stoves which burned sawdust as fuel.

We studied Farsi (Persian) language from a group of Afghan teachers. They also taught us about the culture and customs of Afghanistan, and how to get along.

In our free time, we walked in the bazaars, went exploring by bicycle or taxi, or drank tea and smoked water pipes.

I used to love to go to a laid-back, hippie-type restaurant on "Chicken Street," near the Green Hotel, where a man from India was always playing beautiful music with his sitar.

CHAPTER ONE

The Road to India

The paved road from Istanbul, in western Turkey, continues eastward through Tehran, Iran, through Afghanistan and Pakistan, all the way to New Delhi, India, and beyond. United Nations Highway One is the modern designation for the road. The route itself is one of the most ancient and famous trade routes in the world: the legendary "Overland to India" route.

It is also called "The Silk Road" because of the ancient trade in silk which went from China all the way to Rome. Marco Polo had traveled the Silk Road through Afghanistan in 1272, with his father and uncle. They passed through the spectacular province of Badakhshan—high, forested country, famous for its deep-blue lapis lazuli stones. Then they went through the Wakhan corridor of the Pamirs, the "Roof of the World." The Pamir Mountains are the home of the "Ovis Poli," the huge, wild "Marco Polo" sheep, which look like a gigantic version of Alaskan Dall Sheep. Finally, they climbed through the Wakhjir Pass (16,100 feet), and continued eastward to China.

Now, there were always many young travelers with backpacks, especially from Europe, making the journey from Europe to India, London to Kathmandu, or some variation thereof. Thousands of them passed through Afghanistan every year, by bus, car, motorcycle, or even bicycle! I enjoyed talking with them and envied their freedom and sense of adventure.

After a couple of weeks in Kabul, we were sent eastward to continue our three months of training at a town in the desert called Jalalabad. It was pretty grim. On my first day there, I was sent to take a message concerning vaccinations to a doctor at a hospital. For a hospital, the place was incredibly dusty and filthy, with flies buzzing everywhere. People directed me to the doctor, I knocked on the door, and he told me to enter.

I was astounded when I opened the door and found two very bloody, dead Afghan men lying on the tile floor. It looked like they had both been shot in the face at close range with a shotgun. The Afghan doctor examining them looked up with a big grin and said, "They were stupid! They stopped in the desert to pick up a hitchhiker and he killed them both and stole their truck!" He then threw his head back and laughed as though this were hilarious! I quickly handed him the paper with the message, turned, and left. I was close to vomiting.

A couple of days after that, some of us watched an Afghan man kill his camel with a sword in a fit of rage. He then gutted it, butchered it and sold the meat on the spot. He had plenty of buyers. We also watched people whipping emaciated horses and once saw a group of children stone a stray dog to death. Some Afghans, I was told, hate dogs and consider that dogs breathe out filth with their breath. Although abusing animals like this is strictly forbidden in Islam, some people did not seem to understand.

Well, our training in Jalalabad went okay. The Afghan women, by the way, almost all wore the socklike, complete body covering called the "chador" or "shadri." It was as if each woman were wearing a tent-like contraption which was a full-body veil. It was annoying, at least, not to be able to look at the women.

About women: once we accidentally threw a frisbee over a high mud fence. One male trainee climbed up and looked over into a yard where several women ran into a house. A minute or two later, a very mean-looking Afghan man brandishing a bolt action rifle came striding into our compound. He was bearded, wearing a turban and robes, with a bandolier of rifle cartridges and a very long knife on his belt. He spoke angrily in Farsi, shook his fist in the air repeatedly, and left. One of our male Afghan teachers translated that he said if anyone sticks their head over the fence again, he will kill them.

We didn't play frisbee any more.

Becoming a Peace Corps Volunteer

After the training, we were sworn in as full-fledged Peace Corps Volunteers. I was sent to teach English as a Second Language (ESL) to the Afghan government employees at a place called Central Statistics Office in the Karte Char section of Kabul. The work was okay. My students were pleasant, educated adults and the classes included both men and women. But being a foreigner in Afghanistan was very difficult. Especially for a young person from a Western country, it was exasperating! Afghanistan is a rigidly strict Muslim country, which at that point in time had a repressive, police-state type of government.

There were no bars, no night clubs, no dancing, no alcohol, and so forth. At that time, there was not any television in the country, either. Or videos. And all women were oppressed, sometimes brutally.

Downtown Scene Near Public Garden Bridge, Kabul, Afghanistan

Local bus, Jalalabad, Afghanistan

Historically, foreigners have invaded Afghanistan, plundered and just brought trouble. So many Afghans don't even try to conceal their contempt. One favorite trick is for an Afghan to "accidentally" spit on the pants or dress of a foreigner. The leering smile and phony apology only make it worse. And if you really protest, you stand a good chance of having an icepick-shaped knife plunged into your chest by an irate Afghan male.

Watermelon Bazaar, Herat, Afghanistan. (Marco Polo wrote that Afghanistan has the best melons in the world.)

Incidentally, the word "xenophobia," meaning fear or hatred of strangers or foreigners, is believed by some people to come from the name of one of Alexander the Great's generals, named Xenophon. Alexander and his army passed through Afghanistan in about three hundred B.C. en route to India. (Also, in the vicinity of the Khyber Pass, Alexander and his army were harassed by two flying, "silvery shields" which swooped at them repeatedly. I have always wondered if those were ancient accounts of UFOs.)

In Afghanistan there is more than a ninety per cent illiteracy rate, so there are a lot of uneducated, even stupid people running around. The poverty in Afghanistan is grindingly oppressive. There is no petroleum-based wealth in Afghanistan. There was a tremendous amount of public filth, open sewers and the like. My observation was that there were many Afghan people who unfortunately emit strong body odors because of not enough bathing and clothes washing.

One of the few places where a young American could go to relax and forget about being in Afghanistan was at the American Embassy

Street scene, Herat, Afghanistan

Annex. It became a regular refuge for me in all seasons. And being located in the embassy, alcohol was not illegal.

Within the Annex was a spacious bar, equipped with foreign liquors. The bartender was a Pakistani Christian known simply as Mr.

Wilson. Pakistani Christians are generally obligated to abandon their given family names and take Western names, which is how he ended up with the same name as Dennis the Menace's neighbor in the popular comic strip. And being a Christian, it was okay for him to handle alcoholic beverages, which was forbidden of the Muslims. And so occasionally I would stop by for a beer or two.

Edgar Cayce and the Subject of Jesus in India

I had volunteered for the Peace Corps in the first place, because I was hoping to get a work assignment in India. I embarked on my own journey of spiritual unfolding when at the age of eighteen I met a young man from Hopkinsville, Kentucky who told me about Edgar Cayce (also from Hopkinsville, Kentucky), who is America's best known and best respected psychic and prophet (often called "The Sleeping Prophet" because his many readings were given while in a sleeplike trance).

Among the thousands of life readings and medical readings which Cayce gave, there were numerous times when Cayce stated that Jesus had indeed lived in India. For example, in one trance, Cayce said: "Jesus' studies in India, Persia and Egypt covered much greater periods...." Furthermore, the readings said that Jesus had lived many years in India and had studied and learned from great teachers there. I wanted to investigate this, and I became a member of an Edgar Cayce study group, which I've continued to participate in throughout the years.

A second source of information, **The Aquarian Gospel of Jesus the Christ** by Levi Dowling, a Civil War chaplain in the Union Army, gives a beautiful narrative account of the life and teachings of Jesus in India, Tibet and elsewhere.

Dowling explained that he obtained the material by frequently going into very deep meditation and contacting the Akashic Records, purported to be a recording of all the words, thoughts, and deeds of all the people who have ever lived on earth. Cayce also claimed to have frequently used the Akashic Records, and he affirmed that they are very real! So regarding Jesus in India, I was inclined to be open minded to the idea of the Akashic records as being a possible source of knowledge, if for no other reason than the high regard I have for the Edgar Cayce readings.

A third source of information on this topic was to be found in the writings of Paramahansa Yogananda. Yogananda was sent to the west by Babaji (the rediscoverer of Kriya Yoga, the ancient form of yoga that Krishna imparted to his disciple, Arjuna) and Yogananda's guru, Swami Sri Yukteswar. They defined a mission for him in which he was to spread the teachings of yoga in the Western world and teach about the links that bind the teachings of Hinduism and the ancient science of yoga with the teachings of Christ. Yogananda founded Self-Realization Fellowship in the 1920's, which has become a worldwide mission today, the Church of All Religions that encompasses also the Yogoda Satsanga Society in India (www.srf-yogananda.org).

After the launch of his literary career with his book **Autobiography of a Yogi**, Yogananda proceeded to write many other books, essays and teachings. One of the common themes that recurs again and again in his work is the assertion that Jesus spent years in India between the ages of twelve and thirty. Yogananda insists that the traditions of Jesus' travels in India date back to the centuries immediately following Jesus' lifetime on earth, and that this has been known to sages, rishis and other spiritual teachers throughout India – including knowledge by the office of the Shankaracharya, the "archbishop" or "Pope" of Hinduism. Many claim that the position of Shankaracharya dates to the centuries before the birth of Christ.

All of this provided groundwork for the investigation that has become one of my lifelong quests.

After all, didn't it seem really strange about the mysterious, missing years in the life of Jesus between the ages of twelve and when he began his ministry at the age of thirty? Why is there only one transitional verse between those two ages? That verse is in the second chapter of Luke, and it states: "And Jesus increased in wisdom and stature, and in favor with God and man." And that describes many years of living?!? Jesus of Nazareth is easily the most important historical figure in world history! And we are expected to meekly accept that missing time without explanation, without any question??

Doesn't it seem transparently obvious that something significant is being intentionally omitted? And if so, what could the hot potato be? And what heresies are within the truth which has been concealed from us??

The conventional explanation is that following the incident at the age of twelve, at the feast of the Passover, when Jesus disappeared from Mary and his surrogate father Joseph, he was found in a very scholarly discussion with Rabbi Hillel and the other Jewish high priests and doctors of the law. Later, we are supposed to believe he worked with Joseph in the carpentry shop until his ministry.

Then he began His ministry at age thirty and was crucified at the age of thirty-three. Perhaps as is shown in the movie **"Ben Hur,"** Jesus would frequently skip off from his carpentry work and go for long, moody walks in the hills where somehow, magically, great spiritual knowledge would keep coming to him.

Despite my infinite respect and profound regard for Jesus (and also for William Wyler, the director of **"Ben Hur"**), I think that explanation is downright dopey!

It makes much more sense to me that a person so intensely and deeply dedicated to spiritual growth, as Jesus was, would travel and actively seek out great spiritual teachers who would have the wisdom, training and books he would need.

I was told that the great Muslim traveler, Ibn Batutta, was visited at his deathbed by a group of admirers. They said, "You are the greatest of all travelers." As the story goes, he then sat up, smiled and shook a finger. "No," he replied, "if you learn the truth about Hazrat Issa, Prophet Jesus, you will find that Jesus is King of Travelers." The phrase stuck in my mind. The **Hadith** of the Muslims (sayings of the holy prophet) in fact calls Jesus "Prince of Travelers" and "The Great Traveler."

Wouldn't that indicate that Jesus must have traveled extensively outside of the Middle East? And that Muslim scholars had various historical sources of knowledge about those travels?

Only a few days before my departure for Afghanistan, an amazing incident happened. I strongly believe now that it was an act of divine order, or as Bill Moyers would put it: "being helped by hidden hands." I was staying at my mother's house in our home town of Lampasas, Texas. One afternoon my mother returned to the house in a state of excitement and told me that she had just seen a high school classmate of hers whom she had not seen in many years. This man had become a career diplomat in the U.S. State Department, and, as it turned out, had spent much of his career in India!

Hearing about Kashmir, India

My mother was at a fabric shop in downtown Lampasas that day, buying thread for her dry cleaning business, when she saw an old high school friend and his wife. At first, she walked out of the store, uncertain if the man was really whom she thought. But then somehow, she rallied her courage and walked back into the store and spoke to the man. It was her classmate after all!

Ancient Vertical Windmill, Herat, Afghanistan

He introduced his wife and after a few minutes of reminiscing, my mother happened to mention that her younger son would be leaving in a few days to go to Afghanistan, to serve as a Peace Corps volunteer. She explained that my reason for going to that part of the world was because I had the very keen desire to visit India and to see many parts of India firsthand. Her friend's eyes became big, and he enthusiastically explained that he had spent much of his life living and working in India.

"I must speak with your son!" he exclaimed.

As soon as my mother and I had finished speaking, there came a knock at the door and in stepped my mother's friend. He smiled and we shook hands, and we invited him to sit with us in the breezeway.

While my mother went to the kitchen to bring drinks, her friend discussed India in some detail. Before long, he came to an important point. "You must visit Kashmir while you are in India!" he insisted. "There is no other place like it," he explained. "On the whole planet it is unique. The vale of Kashmir is like heaven on earth."

My mother's friend soon had to leave, but I thought a long time about what he had said. Inwardly, something had changed.

Caretaker with doves at the Tomb of Ali in Mazar-i-Sharif, Afghanistan

Before, I had thought only marginally about Kashmir. It was on a far, back burner. Probably, I would not have gone there. But thanks to my mother's friend, I had made a decision: I would go to Kashmir, God willing. I am very glad I did. I would never have expected what I found there!

Murree Beer

To return to my Peace Corps experience in Afghanistan: one afternoon after work, I was at the bar within the American Embassy Annex. As I walked to the bar and approached the Pakistani bartender, Mr. Wilson, I had no idea that something significant was about to take place in my life. I looked behind Mr. Wilson at the display bottles sitting on the shelves.

One bottle of beer in particular caught my attention.

The label said "Murree Beer," a brand brewed in neighboring Pakistan.

I asked to see a bottle. As I examined the label, I asked Mr. Wilson where the name Murree came from.

"Murree is a town in northern Pakistan in the Himalayan foothills, sahib," replied Mr. Wilson.

"Is Murree named after an Englishman?" I asked.

"Oh, no, sahib," he responded, "Murree comes from the name Mary."

"Was Mary a woman from England?"

"Oh, no, sahib. Mary was the mother of Jesus," he said.

I felt puzzled. I took a long sip of beer. "But Pakistan is mostly a Muslim country. Why would a town have a Christian name?" I asked.

"Because Mary is buried there; her tomb is in that place. The town grew up around it and is named for Mary," he said.

My mind was boggled for a long moment. I took a longer sip of beer. "Let me see if I understand you correctly," I said. "You are saying that Mary, the mother of Jesus Christ, is buried at a place in northern Pakistan. Is that correct?" I asked.

"Most assuredly, sahib. I have been there numerous times myself and visited the holy tomb. It is considered a sacred place by both Christians and Muslims alike."

"But why would Mary, the mother of Jesus, be buried in northern Pakistan? What would she possibly be doing there?" I asked.

Mr. Wilson shrugged his shoulders and took a deep breath as he dried a glass with a towel. "Some people believe that Jesus survived the crucifixion; that he was in a state of near-death. They believe that he later returned to India and was accompanied by his mother and other people. Mary became sick and died during the journey." Mr. Wilson turned to take care of another customer and I shifted my thoughts inward and reflected on our discussion. How could this be?

Independent Evidence from Herat, Afghanistan

It was years later when I was reading *Jesus in India* by Dr. James W. Deardorff that I found a passage on page 245 concerning the existence of a Yuz Asaf sect near Herat, Afghanistan. Yuz Asaf is said to be the name used by Jesus after the crucifixion and means "leader of the healed" (or cleansed). Specifically, the name may refer to those who were healed of leprosy. This sect knew of Yuz Asaf having survived the crucifixion and traveling past their area at or near Herat and on to the Kashmir area.

They also knew of his time spent as a youth in India. This is completely independent evidence from any which the Ahmadiyyas (an Islamic sect of Indian origin) have recorded, and so is quite valuable.

The passage states: "In northwestern Afghanistan there are some one thousand devotees of Issa, son of Maryam, living within several scattered villages and centered at Herat. They revere him as having been Yuz Asaf, their ancient teacher. Their traditions are surprisingly similar to what is reported herein: Issa escaped the cross, was helped to flee to India, where he had been before in his youth, and later settled in Kashmir where he lived for over thirty years past the time of the crucifixion. He was (again) regarded as possessing the power to perform miracles. These believers in Issa are not Ahmadiyyas, however, as they possess their own traditions on this that date back through the centuries."

The passage continues: "Their present leader, Abba Yahiyya (Father John) can recite the names of the succession of their other leaders or teachers through nearly sixty generations back to Yuz Asaf himself, according to O.M. Burke, who personally interviewed Father John while researching Sufism in this area of the globe (Omar Michael Burke, **Among the Dervishes**, London: Octogon Press, 1976, p. 107). If one assigns thirty-two years per generation, this number of generations indeed takes one back to the end of the first century. Burke referred to the sect as Christians, as they do regard Issa as the Son of God; however, they cannot be considered Christians in any orthodox sense. They do not trust the New Testament Gospels, for example, as their own traditions were learned from Issa or Yuz Asaf during years following the crucifixion, according to their leader."

The passage concludes: "In eastern Afghanistan near the towns of Ghazni and Jalalabad, respectively, there are two platforms that bear the name of Yuz Asaf, where he is said to have sat and preached (K.N. Ahmad, **Heaven on Earth**, p. 360; Kersten, **Jesus Lived in India**, p. 184). Unfortunately, K.N. Ahmed did not spell out the locations of the platforms within either of these two cities, nor in this instance did he refer to his sources.

Returning to my Peace Corps experience: I thanked Mr. Wilson for our good discussion, finished my beer and left him a good tip. Then I walked to the far side of the mostly vacant room and found a dimly lit area with cushions beside a wall where I could lie down for a while.

Waiting for His Divine Cue

Wow, I thought, that was a very strange bottle of beer! *"How do you like your Jesus"?* I thought.

Well, I thought then, I like my Jesus stone-cold dead. That is, after he's been crucified. Then he gets to come back to life magically for a little while—the Resurrection! Of course, it's kind of peculiar that he still needs to eat food, like when he visited the fishermen and said he was hungry and ate some fish.

And after he's appeared to enough folks, and given the Great Commission to preach the Gospel everywhere, he miraculously ascends into the air (or was that added later?) and sits at the right hand of God Almighty. And supposedly, he's still sitting there now, biding his time, waiting for his divine cue, to go into action at the Second Coming. That was the way I liked my Jesus. That was the way I'd always thought of him.

Certainly, I did not want Jesus to be in a state of near-death when taken down from the cross, and then with the help of healers, medicines and salves, to survive in a physical rather than a supernatural way! And certainly, like any good Christian, I didn't want him to become healthy again! And, God forbid, I wouldn't want him later to run off to India. And be a pal to his Hindu and Buddhist friends! Maybe drinking wine together! And later getting to die, like any normal human being! And being buried in the ground! Who did he think he was? Didn't he know we had put him on a very, very high pedestal? And raised him to God status? (More on this in Chapter Eleven: How Do You Like Your Jesus?)

Yes, I was raised as a Fundamentalist, Protestant Christian, and even though as a teenager I had begun to believe in reincarnation, I was still clinging tightly to the basic package of what I had been taught. I immediately put up a mental shield when I was confronted with something that disputed what was comfortable.

But that tomb of Mary! How wildly improbable! Who could have dreamed up such an absurd location! And the story that went with it! How bizarre can you get? *But what was the explanation for Mary's tomb being in Pakistan?*

I didn't realize it at the time, but as I prepared to go from Afghanistan on vacation to India, more pieces of the puzzle were about to fall into place.

In the Corridors around the Golden Temple, Amritsar, Punjab, India

2. Journey to the Vale of Kashmir: Heaven on Earth

> *Go confidently in the direction of your dreams;*
> *live the life you have imagined.*
> —Henry David Thoreau

On a crisp, sunny morning in the beginning of October, 1974, I put on my Kelty backpack, said farewell to my housemate, and I walked out onto Chicken Street in Kabul, Afghanistan. I soon hailed a taxi, negotiated a price, and was on my way to the Silver Bullet, the well-known direct bus from Kabul to Peshawar, Pakistan. Our route lay through the fabled Khyber Pass, the most famous of the more than three hundred passes through the Hindu Kush, the "Hindu Killer" mountains which separated ancient India from Afghanistan.

The Silver Bullet didn't actually travel at great speed, but it was silver-colored, and the name was catchy. I was already having an immensely good time, as I watched the spectacular mountain scenery and listened to the exotic sitar and drum music on the radio. I was on my way to India! I had embarked on a great adventure which years before I had dreamed about, but which now was becoming a joyful reality.

I reflected back, thinking about the hard years of study, and my graduation from the University of Alaska at Fairbanks. I remembered how my father had died from a heart attack in our native Texas when I was nineteen years old. I recalled how we had hunted together so much and had always had our big dream of driving together some summer, going up the Alaska Highway, having a big adventure together in Alaska. Seeing it with our own eyes!

As a teenager and young man, my father often read books by Jack London, such as **White Fang** and **The Call of the Wild**. He also had a book of poems, which I still have, written by Robert Service, called **The Spell of the Yukon**. Service was a Canadian bank teller who wrote poems about the far north. He is often called "The Bard of the North." Two of his most famous poems are "The Cremation of Sam McGee" and "The Shooting of Dan McGrew." In the summertime, at a village near Fairbanks, Alaska called Ester, there are daily performances of his poems. The place is called The Malamute Saloon. Dad would have loved it!

However, during the last few years of his life, Dad had increasingly debilitating heart disease, and our Alaska plans had to be put on hold. It was a couple of months after Dad's death that a friend and I departed Texas to drive up to Alaska in late May that year. We drove in the pickup-camper my father had given me. I was nineteen years old at the time.

Fighting Forest Fires

We were hired that summer in Alaska to fight forest fires with the Bureau of Land Management (BLM). In fact, we were hired the same day we arrived! I had a lot of adventures! Once, during my second summer of fighting forest fires, a friend and I almost got burned to death when the wind changed suddenly and hit us with a wall of dense smoke and flames.

The wind whipped erratically as we dropped to the ground. For several long, terror-stricken moments we were confused and blinded

A BLM fire crew prepares to fight a forest fire in interior Alaska

by the dense smoke; the popping, hissing inferno seemed to surround us. The heat was terrifying! And it was closing in. By chance, we found that the area six inches or closer to the ground was relatively free of smoke. Finally, we found a clear route and crawled swiftly to safety.

The author at the summit of Mt. Kilimanjaro, Tanzania (19,340 feet)

I enrolled in the University of Alaska at Fairbanks, and after some years graduated with a B.A. degree in Speech Communications. I minored in Secondary Education and got a teacher certification. Incidentally, at UAF, I learned to skydive and made nineteen parachute jumps. Also, about a year before I graduated, I made a summertime trip to East Africa, spending six weeks in Kenya, Tanzania and Uganda. During that trip, I joined a climbing team and went to the summit of Mt. Kilimanjaro (19,340 feet). That was a five-day climb. Later, I went to Ngorongoro Crater (shown in the opening scenes of the John Wayne movie **"Hatari"**), the Serengheti Plains, and other fantastic places. I had a wonderful time!

During the five-day climb of Kilimanjaro, it turned out that three of the dozen climbers were American Peace Corps volunteers!

We talked for hours about the Peace Corps and its accomplishments. One of the volunteers, Buff MacKenzie, invited me to visit his school in Mwatate, Kenya, which I did.

Back in Alaska, I threw myself into my senior year of studies at the University. During that time, I applied to enter the Peace Corps. Also, during the winter, I began preparations to join a climbing team that would make a summer ascent of Mt. McKinley (Denali).

The author (right) with Gregory Craig and Bob Carlson at the summit of Mt. McKinley (Denali), Alaska, 20,320 feet

I graduated in May that year and began the climb the following month. Ray Genet was our leader. We reached the summit on the fourteenth day (20,320 feet), and it took us six days to descend. In later times, I used to visit Ray at his cabin in Talkeetna. Years later, Ray Genet died after reaching the summit of Mount Everest, in Nepal. Ray's body, I have heard, is still up there on Everest at around 28,000 feet, in the "death zone."

I wonder if Ray is smiling?

Ray Genet holds Marlene Titus in a playful moment on Mt. McKinley, Alaska. Genet's body now rests eternally at 28,000 feet on Mr. Everest

After climbing Mt. McKinley, I accepted the invitation to join the Peace Corps and went to Afghanistan. (Later, I was assigned by the Peace Corps to the Fiji Islands in the South Pacific, where almost every day after my teaching work was finished, I would go diving on the nearby coral reefs. But that is getting ahead in my story.)

The Legendary Khyber Pass

Now I was on a bus winding through the Khyber Pass, bound for Pakistan and ultimately India and Nepal! Life was good!

The Khyber Pass, from one end to the other, is actually about fourteen miles or so in length. Austere warning signs at both entrances to the pass advise travelers that under no circumstances should anyone attempt to spend the night in the region. After dark, there are many groups of smugglers, bandits and just plain low-life cut-throats who will gleefully kill someone just to steal a wristwatch. At night, the Khyber Pass is one of the most dangerous places on the planet, and it should be avoided then.

The bus rolled into Peshawar, Pakistan, just about lunchtime. It was a dusty, sunny autumn day as we moved slowly through an amusing menagerie of camels, donkeys, horses, water buffaloes and human caretakers wearing turbans and baggy clothing. I would have to be careful where I stepped!

Shouldering my Kelty backpack, I walked into the crowded bus station to ask how to get to the train station. It looked like I was the only Westerner in the room. A turbaned, strong-looking man was issuing tickets and speaking in Farsi (Persian) with someone. I could understand some of what he was saying. Apparently, he was from Landi Kotal, a Pakistani frontier town near the Khyber Pass, which has a notoriously large gun bazaar and a wild west type of atmosphere. Within reach of his left hand was a Remington model 700 bolt action rifle.

Upon seeing me, he smiled and nodded and courteously directed me to the train station. I took one of the local three-wheeled taxi scooters and soon arrived at the station. Earlier, I had thought about spending the night in Peshawar, at the inexpensive Khyber Hotel in Saddar Bazaar. On weekend trips I had stayed there before. But I decided to keep the momentum of my journey going; I would go on the evening train to Rawalpindi and Lahore. Besides, the all night train ride would save me the cost of a hotel and get me closer to my destination.

Nanga Parbat and the Baltoro Glacier

I briefly met a couple of my Peace Corps friends from Afghanistan at the train station in Rawalpindi. These two young men were on vacation and were headed north to Skardu, Pakistan and ultimately to trek on the Baltoro Glacier in the direction of K-2, the second highest mountain in the world. The flight from Skardu would take them near Nanga Parbat (Naked Mountain), a famous and beautiful Himalayan peak whose steep slopes are often swept clean by avalanches.

As the call came to reboard the train, they told me about anti-American riots that had been going on locally because a newsletter from the American Embassy had contained a small drawing of the prophet Mohammed. Of course, the newsletter had only been intended for American personnel, but a copy had fallen into Pakistani hands and was circulated. For Muslims, any drawing or image of Muhammed is a sacrilege, so outraged crowds of Pakistanis were attacking and beating any American they could find. My friends were disguised ("in mufti"), dressed like hooded locals and also wearing blankets; they planned to slip out of Rawalpindi that night and head north to Skardu. I shook hands and bade them farewell, promising to see them back in Afghanistan. I was glad to get back aboard the train and be leaving Rawalpindi!

Early the next morning, the train pulled into the Lahore station amid a tumult of noise and activity. I shouldered my backpack and made my way through a troupe of dancing beggars and found a bicycle-rickshaw driver who would take me to the Asia Hotel, a modestly priced place with air conditioning. It was autumn, but the heat and humidity were oppressive.

As I checked into the hotel, the clerk asked me in a pleasant way where was I going? He was writing information into a ledger. For a moment, I was not sure what to say. In those days, there was very bad blood between Pakistan and India. After several awkward seconds, the clerk leaned compassionately forward and whispered:

"Are you going to India?" he asked.

"Yes," I replied honestly.

"Very well," he said, "I shall write that you are going to Wagah, Pakistan, a border town on the way."

I thanked the helpful clerk and headed up to my room. After a shower and a change of clothes, I headed out to visit the Lahore Museum.

The Zam Zam, a huge and ornate cannon which Rudyard Kipling wrote about in his classic **Kim**, sits impressively in front of the museum. I touched the enormous weapon and marveled at some of the colorful, exotic history which actually happened in that part of the world.

Inside the Lahore Museum, I was particularly interested in seeing a famous statue of the Fasting Buddha. This exquisitely made piece of art depicts how Guatama Siddhartha, the Buddha, looked as he neared the end of many days of fasting, sitting beneath the tree of enlightenment, the Bodhi Tree.

The next morning I was on my way to Wagah. I stepped out of the dusty bus and passed through Pakistani Customs. Then with the other travelers, I shouldered my backpack and walked about four hundred yards through a no-man's-land buffer zone to reach the border of India. A long line of turbaned men carried boxes of grapes on their heads. Tall, fragrant eucalyptus trees swayed gently in the sunny, morning breeze. The dry earth was a reddish-orange color.

A young man from a small town in Texas, from a modest background, I had always wanted to see exotic India with my own eyes. And now here I was! I had made it!

Arriving in India

I smiled broadly and said a cheerful "Hello" as I handed my passport to the Indian Customs official.

He nodded stoically, noticing my beaming grin, and traded sidelong glances with some of the other customs officials. As he found my India visa and stamped it, he asked if everything was all right.

I assured him yes, and I told him that I was just delighted to be visiting India. He cast a few more sideways glances as he handed me my passport, said "Welcome to India" and waved me through.

Several buses were waiting nearby for the short trip to Amritsar, capital of the province of Punjab. Amritsar, meaning "pool of nectar," is the holiest city of the Sikh religion, a spiritual path started by Guru Nanak in the 15th century.

The provincial name "Punjab" means "Five Rivers" or five waters (panch ab) in the Punjabi language.

Journey to the Vale of Kashmir: Heaven on Earth

I checked into a small hotel, booked passage on a bus to depart the next morning for Srinagar, and I found a bicycle-rickshaw with a sun shade.

The driver was a pleasant man and we made a deal for a tour of Amritsar which would include a stopover at the Golden Temple of the Sikhs. Some tourists decline using rickshaws because they think they are dehumanizing, or something like that. Then the drivers don't have any business and go hungry! That is <u>really</u> dehumanizing!

The drivers appreciate the business, and, of course, if you're going up a steep hill you can use your common sense by getting off and walking to the top with the driver.

Crossing the border from Wagah, Pakistan, into India

At the Golden Temple of the Sikhs

At the Enclosure Entrance to the Golden Temple, I gave my driver money for a soft drink and told him to wait outside in the cool shade. At the entrance I read the instructions which basically said that everyone is welcome and the rules are: everyone must remove footwear and socks and wash feet at the entrance (a steady flow of cool, clear water through a depressed area in the white marble floor made this easy), everyone must have a head covering of some sort (a helpful

Sikh told me I could tie my red bandana pirate-style on my head and that would be acceptable), everyone must bring an offering of flowers (many flower shops and vendors are within a few steps; I bought a small bundle), and lastly, no one may use tobacco products, drugs or alcohol within the temple grounds.

I was ready!

With a smile, I joined the flow of Sikh pilgrims and stepped into the entrance.

After a few steps, the entrance opened into a large, open-air enclosure perhaps about the size of four football fields. Most of the area was a large, shallow pool of water (considered the amrit, or pool of nectar) in which a white, marble walkway led to the center.

At the Golden Temple of the Sikhs, Amritsar, Punjab Province, India

In the center of the pool was the Golden Temple! In the bright afternoon sun it was spectacular!

In one corner of the surrounding courtyard, there is a perpetual soup kitchen, of sorts, a charitable feeding place open at all hours, day and night, for anyone who needed a meal. I returned later in the afternoon and had a tasty barley-lentils soup with tortilla-like chappatis. It was good! I was impressed by the generosity and industriousness of the Sikhs.

Inside the Golden Temple

Walking slowly, I followed the flow of pilgrims and went on the walkway into the Golden Temple. A wonderful, jasmine-scented incense wafted out of the large open doors. Many of the entering Sikhs laid face down on the marble floor, in a posture of complete prostration, showing their reverence at being in such a holy place.

I walked upstairs, where within glass enclosures, elderly Sikh holy men are constantly sitting and reading out loud from ornate copies of the Sikh holy book, the Granth. I was deeply moved and impressed that the Sikhs would be so open and willing to share the most sacred place of their religion, even with a non-Sikh "Infidel" such as myself.

Only about three years before that time, en route to East Africa, I had a three-day stopover in Rome and had gone inside St. Peter's Basilica in the Vatican. I'm not Catholic (in this lifetime) but I was welcome there, also. For me, St. Peter's was impressive but dreadfully serious, cold and austere (the white marble Pieta added to the somber mood). The mood in the Golden Temple, by contrast, seemed joyful, yet serious, like a spiritual celebration.

The next morning I was riding the bus to Pathankot and from there to Jammu, in the Himalayan foothills. After a hot, mosquito-infested night at a cheap hotel, I left Jammu on the bus that would take me to Kashmir, all the way to Srinagar. The scenery was spectacular as the bus bounced and swayed on the precarious mountain roads, negotiating hairpin turns and passing near cascading waterfalls.

Finally, late in the afternoon, we ascended a mountainside and approached the entrance of a huge, concrete tunnel where we paused a few moments. The letters above the entrance said:

WELCOME TO THE VALE OF KASHMIR
HEAVEN ON EARTH

We passed through the tunnel, and there below us lay a beautiful green valley with forests and lakes and craggy, snow-capped Himalayan peaks on either side. An abundance of sweet-smelling wildflowers were on both sides of the road. So this was Kashmir! I was glad I had listened to my mother's high school friend and decided to come here.

Nearing sunset, the bus pulled into the station in Srinagar. I unloaded my Kelty backpack and took a seat in the station to think over my next move. My Berlitz guidebook suggested that one of the many houseboats in Srinagar could be an interesting place to stay.

I watched in amusement as Indian tourists from other parts of India were being hustled and sweet-talked by hotel employees, houseboat owners and taxi drivers. Mostly they were speaking in English, because it is often considered a neutral, common language, whereas Hindi, the national language, is mostly spoken in the northern half of India.

A dignified, neatly dressed man wearing a shirt and slacks walked up to me and said "Is sahib looking for hotel accomodation?"

I pressed both of my open hands together, palm to palm, in front of my chest in the traditional greeting, smiled and said "Namaste." Literally, the greeting means "I salute the divinity within you."

The man smiled broadly and gave the same greeting.

"Yes," I replied, "I am looking for a place to stay." He then told me that he was the owner of a beautiful houseboat called the Mount

Houseboat scene, Srinagar, Kashmir, India

Everest, and that it was nearby on the Jhellum River, in the area called the Bund. And for a modest sum, I could have a room with breakfast included. Soon, we were walking on our merry way to the Mount Everest. I turned in early after dinner that evening, breathing the sweet aroma of flower blossoms as the houseboat rocked gently in the water. And so, I thought, this is the Vale of Kashmir!

After a delightful breakfast of eggs, toast with jelly, fresh fruit and Darjeeling tea, I decided to stay there at least two or three nights. I felt somehow intrigued by the area and that I should investigate and learn more, even if my visit were brief. Kashmir is like a real-life Shangri La, incredibly beautiful and charming.

Ahead on my journey, I had planned a very ambitious itinerary: a visit to the Tibetan refugee community at Dharamsala, India, then on to New Delhi, the capital. Next, to Agra, to visit the Taj Mahal. Then onward by train to Varanasi (Benares), the holiest city of the Hindus, on the magnificent and sacred Ganges River. Then northward to the spectacular Himalayan Kingdom of Nepal.

After preparations in Kathmandu, I would be walking for twenty days, or so, to reach Namche Bazaar and then to the base camp of Mt. Everest. Later, from an airstrip at Lukla, I would fly back to Kathmandu. Finally, I would visit Pokhara, in western Nepal, see the Annapurna peaks, also Dhaulagiri, and Machapuchare (Fishtail Mountain), and then return to Afghanistan.

Hand-Operated Small Ferris Wheel, Jalalabad, Afghanistan

The Taj Mahal. Agra, India

3. A Meeting with the Author of *Christ in Kashmir*

Follow your bliss.
—Joseph Campbell

That sunny, autumn morning in Srinagar I felt the intuitive pull to find a bookstore. I walked out of the houseboat and under some nearby shade trees, where I could see a taxi was parked. The driver was reading a newspaper. I took that as a good sign. It was.

The driver was friendly and spoke good English. I told him I was looking for a good bookstore, which would have a lot of books in English. He smiled and said that he knew of just such a bookstore and that it was not a long drive. I asked how many rupees the drive would cost. The driver said fifteen, I offered ten, we settled on twelve and were off.

The bookstore was in a quiet part of the city. This was well before the fierce military conflict was unleashed between Muslims and Hindus that has made Kashmir a land of bombs and war. For many years, it was a much more tranquil place.

As I entered and looked around, I saw it had a laid-back and rustic kind of 1950's atmosphere. Ancient ceiling fans squeaked softly, and the owner, a middle-aged man wearing european clothes with a necktie, sat reading a book near the cash register. A steaming cup of tea was at his side. I looked around and saw that I was the only customer. That was fine with me.

I browsed around in the front part of the bookstore for a minute or two. There were some books in English, yes, but nothing of much interest. Then I turned and found a display of yellow-colored books near the front of the store. The thing that got my attention was a drawing on the book cover which showed Jesus Christ on the cross and the title in large letters: **Christ in Kashmir**. Below the title was the author's name: Aziz Kashmiri, Honors in Urdu and Literature, Editor Urdu Daily Roshni, Srinagar, Kashmir.

I picked up the book, glanced through it, and I stared at it again in wonder. It was as though many pieces of a puzzle were beginning to fall into place. What Edgar Cayce had repeatedly said in his trance readings, that Jesus had indeed lived and studied in India. What Levi

Dowling, the Union Army Chaplain, had written about in ***The Aquarian Gospel of Jesus the Christ***, telling about the time that Jesus had lived in Kashmir, and elsewhere, in India. The strange occurrence about my mother's long-lost friend and his mysterious insistence that I must go to Kashmir. And, of course, the very strange bottle of beer from Murree, Pakistan, which brought about the bizarre revelation from Mr. Wilson: that Mary, the mother of Jesus, is buried in northern Pakistan! And that Jesus had survived the crucifixion and lived much of his life in Kashmir!

Could everything be merely a coincidence??? Or in my search for hidden truth, could I have been about to find much more than I had ever imagined? I held the book in my hand then and wondered: should I take the next step? Should I follow my bliss?

I walked over to the shop owner and gave a friendly "Namaste" greeting with my palms placed together. The gentleman placed his book down and returned the greeting with a beaming smile. After paying for **Christ in Kashmir**, I asked the owner if by any chance he might know the author personally? He smiled broadly again and said "Oh yes, Aziz Kashmiri is a good friend of mine." Whereupon, I explained that I was a young American visiting India, with a keen interest in the subject of Jesus in India. And I wondered if I might possibly be able to visit with the author and discuss the subject?

The Daily Roshni

"Well, he is the editor of the Daily Roshni, a newspaper here in Srinagar," said the shop owner, "Let me give him a phone call and see if he is in his office." He picked up a heavy, black 1950's telephone and dialed a number. For a few moments he spoke in Kashmiri, then handed me the phone and said, "He will speak with you." I introduced myself and repeated what I had told the bookstore owner.

"How about right now?" he said, "I have just finished a meeting and I have some free time."

"Yes," I replied, "that is fine; I will be there shortly."

I handed the phone back to the shop owner and asked if he could write directions to the Daily Roshni and tell me a fair price for a taxi. He nodded, wrote quickly in Kashmiri, handed me the paper, and said, "About twelve rupees would be a fair price." We smiled and shook hands, and I thanked him for his help and said farewell.

A Meeting with the Author of "Christ in Kashmir"

I stepped outside the bookstore, and under the shade trees was parked the same taxi which had brought me there! The driver was relaxing and reading his newspaper again. This time I noticed he was reading the Daily Roshni. We smiled at each other and I handed him

the piece of paper with directions. He nodded and I said," Twelve rupees?" He smiled and nodded and motioned for me to get in.

We headed in what seemed to me to be a northeasterly direction, and we were soon going up a hillside. The buildings were mostly white-colored, like white stucco or whitewashed adobe. The taxi stopped on the hillside among some white buildings. "You are here, sahib," said the driver. I paid him, gave him a tip and thanked him. "Good luck, sahib," he said, and then he drove away.

I looked around among the buildings and in the narrow street and realized I couldn't read anything. All the street signs and building signs, both letters and numbers, were in the Kashmiri language. Well, I have strong faith in divine order, and I certainly didn't believe that God was just going to dump me and leave me there for no purpose. So I relaxed, took a few deep breaths and just waited.

Within a few seconds, some children came running and laughing from an alleyway. They spotted me and ran up close, staring in amusement and catching their breath. Soon there were more children, standing there smiling and looking at me in silence. I was thankful they were not throwing rocks or yelling obscenities. I have seen that sort of behavior in some other parts of the world. But these children were respectful; they even wore clean clothes.

Meeting Aziz Kashmiri

I smiled, held up both hands and said slowly in English: "Does anyone know where I can find Aziz Kashmiri?" A well-mannered boy wearing white clothes, who looked to be about six years old, raised his hand straight up, as if he were in school. I pointed at him and he said, "He is my father; I will take you to him."

"Let's go," I said.

We headed off at a brisk walk through a maze of narrow passageways and corridors. Then we ascended some stairs that went up the side of one of the white stucco buildings. We went through a door and entered a large, rustic kind of office with hardwood floors. Most of the north wall was composed of windows of a peculiar kind of wood and glass framework. The view through the windows was a breathtaking panorama of the jagged, glistening ice peaks of the Himalayas. A large desk was near the windows, and two gentlemen wearing European-type clothing were in conversation there.

I thanked the boy who brought me there and gave him a piece

of candy from my jacket pocket. He said thanks and scampered out of the room. The older of the two men pointed at a piece of paper and spoke softly to the younger man, who nodded and left the room. The older man then took several steps toward me, smiled warmly and extended his right hand. "Are you Mr. Martin?" he asked.

"Yes," I replied and shook his hand.

"I am Aziz Kashmiri, editor of the Daily Roshni," he said. He gestured for me to sit in the chair in front of his desk. "Would you like some tea?" he asked.

Aziz Kashmiri

"Yes, I would," I replied.

He clapped his hands softly and asked a servant, who appeared in the doorway to bring us tea.

Later, over steaming cups of tea, we had a far-ranging discussion about the subject of Jesus in India. To my surprise, I found out that in India itself there is a very ancient tradition and folklore that Jesus did indeed live in India. *Moreover, the tradition states that Jesus was in India for two separate long periods of time!* And these were, firstly, the teenage and twenties years of learning and preparation, and secondly, his return sometime after the crucifixion and spending the remainder of his life in India. Mr. Kashmiri even showed me a written statement made by Jawaharlal Nehru, the first Prime Minister of India, concerning his belief in the tradition that Jesus had lived in India.

During our discussion, Mr. Kashmiri mentioned that the tomb of Jesus Christ is in Kashmir and it can be visited by the public! My mind reeled for a while at that one! Why hadn't we ever heard or seen anything about that in the United States!?! (I will discuss this with the reader in abundant detail later, in the chapter toward the end of this book entitled "How Do You Like Your Jesus?")

Mr. Kashmiri went on to explain that the local name used for the tomb is Yuz Asaf, meaning the "Leader of the Cleansed." (At the tomb the name is spelled Youz Asouf, but in the literature and records it more often appears as Yuz Asaf in the English spelling.)

Two stone carvings at the tomb, showing the man's feet, indicate that he had been crucified. An excellent amount of corroborative research identifying Yuz Asaf as Jesus is to be found in Holger Kersten's book: ***Jesus Lived in India***.

I was told in later years, that some people believe that the actual tomb of Jesus is located a few miles outside of Srinagar, on a mountainside at a secret location, where it will not be disturbed. It is said that the Yuz Asaf tomb in the Rozabal section of the Old City is the "public access" location which everyone can reach easily, even physically handicapped people. Many researchers disagree with this, including Suzanne Olsson (author of ***Jesus in Kashmir: The Lost Tomb***). She was told by the locals that the prophet's remains are hidden behind a wall in the tomb, on a ledge. She almost obtained access and approval for DNA testing, but her efforts fell victim at the last moment to acts of terrorism nearby, and she reports that official permission that had been granted was abruptly withdrawn.

The Hemis Monastery at Leh in Ladakh

Aziz Kashmiri also told an intriguing, firsthand story which is a real hot potato! During the 1960's, he had been invited to join a group of other Indian journalists to visit a frequently off-limits area in northern Kashmir called Ladakh. Once there, his group had gone to the rarely visited Hemis Monastery near the town of Leh.

I remembered that Levi Dowling had mentioned in the ***Aquarian Gospel of Jesus the Christ*** that Jesus had spent about two months in that region after leaving Tibet. (The current monastery there, though hundreds of years old, dates from after the lifetime of Jesus, and there is no conclusive information establishing a Buddhist monastery at that location during the days of Christ, though the existence of such an ancient monastery at the site has been widely speculated. Many ancient items, both written records and art, were re-located to Hemis from Tibet during the hundreds of years of the existence of the Hemis Gompa, or monastery.)

At Hemis, the Buddhist priest giving them a tour had explained to Aziz Kashmiri that because the Chief Abbot had recently died, it would be possible for them to enter and look around in the Archives, in the Monastery's basement area. But, when the new Abbot would be chosen, the Archives would be closed again to the public, for years or even decades.

As Mr. Kashmiri walked around the ancient, dusty corridors, shining his flashlight, he glanced at huge stacks of Tibetan documents and hundreds of portraits. The portraits were drawings made in color on thin slabs of stone. The colors, whether oil paints or some other substance, were clear and vivid, although they were obviously very old. Almost all the drawings were of monks with shaved heads, wearing red or orange robes, sitting in the lotus position.

The Unusual Portrait Aziz Kashmiri Saw

However, one drawing was very different! It showed a very robust-looking man with a full head of fairly long hair and a full beard! The hair and beard were of a reddish-brown color, the man was smiling and wearing a brimless, simple cap on his head, similar to the kind of cap that Nehru sometimes wore. He was wearing the traditional, baggy pants and shirt of the region, and a warm-looking vest. He looked strong and had the appearance of a man frequently outdoors. He seemed to be perhaps in his mid-to-late twenties.

Puzzled, Mr. Kashmiri found the monk giving the tour and asked if he knew who that portrait depicted. The monk squatted down, pointed his flashlight at the base of the drawing, and he rubbed off a layer of dust with his fingers. He blew a little, squinted and began to mouth some sounds to himself. The monk had difficulty sounding out the name, but said it was something like "Yashosh "and that the remainder of the writing was something to the effect: "traveling Hebrew scholar and holy man who visited this region during the time of..." The monk remarked that the time frame was about 2,000 years ago.

Mr. Kashmiri's mind reeled! He concluded that this was likely a portrait of Jesus Christ himself! And apparently it was made while Jesus was sitting right in front of the artist, posing for the picture! Wouldn't millions of dedicated Christians all over the world be keenly interested in seeing such a picture?

It happened that the flash unit for Mr. Aziz's camera was broken at that time. He asked the monk several times for permission to take the portrait outside, into the sunlight, but each time the monk refused. Soon thereafter, the tour came to an end, the doors of the Archives were locked, and Mr. Kashmiri was never able to return. A new Abbot was chosen shortly after that time.

I asked Mr. Kashmiri if he knew of anyone since that time who might have seen that drawing? He said that, to his knowledge, he did not know of anyone who had seen it. Nor did he even know if the Archives had been opened since then.

We sat in silence, drinking our steaming tea for some time. My own mind was boggled in a sort of pleasant and profound way.

I thought about the implications of all this. Could it possibly be that out of the billion living Christians on planet Earth, that I myself might be putting together the pieces of an important puzzle in a unique way? Gradually, I was beginning to see "gross consistencies" as I researched more and more about Jesus in India.

In my own mind, I had already come to grips with the conclusion that Jesus really had lived in India. The concept which was harder for me to accept was that Jesus had somehow survived the crucifixion, later recuperated, returned to India, married and had children. Or that he had died in his very old age and been buried in a tomb here in Srinagar.

In my case, it took me about twenty years of spiritual growth, and the accompanying wisdom, strength and flexibility to finally understand and make peace with this concept – and by "make peace" I mean that, barring the possibility of coming across any very convincing, disconfirming proof in the future, I have come to accept it.

From my viewpoint now, those events just mentioned do nothing to diminish the tremendous importance of the life and teachings of Jesus. However, I had concluded that the historical facts of his life had been enshrouded in myth following the crucifixion, and the myth became reality for the billion or more people who lived during the two thousand years that followed and called themselves Christians. Later, I learned that the post-crucifixion passages of the Gospel of Mark were added much later. (Mark is thought by most scholars to be the oldest of the four canonical accounts – Matthew, Mark, Luke and John. The oldest existing ancient manuscript of Mark ends with Mary Magdalene finding Jesus' tomb empty and has nothing about the resurrection or Jesus' appearance to the Apostles three days after the crucifixion. See **The Bible Fraud** by Tony Bixby, pp. 200-201.)

A Lifetime of Research about Jesus in India

I stood up to stretch my legs and walked over to a case of bookshelves a few steps away from Mr. Kashmiri's desk. It was perhaps as high as the top of my head or a little higher and maybe four feet wide. It appeared to be entirely filled with books about subjects related to Jesus in India! Perhaps half of the books had been printed in India, and many of them were in English. Many others were in foreign languages. Some were in exotic tongues. Many of the books looked quite old, but according to Mr. Kashmiri, they all seemed to have some relation to the subject of Jesus in India. I marveled at the books and examined a few of them. There were also large stacks of typewritten materials on the subject.

I could see by the evidence of all that literature that I was by no means the first person to pursue the trail of inquiry on this subject. However, from Murree Beer onward, probably I had stumbled onto this inquiry in a much more unusual way than most.

I turned to Mr. Kashmiri and asked: "Why is the subject of Jesus in India so important to you personally?"

He straightened up in his chair, then took a deep breath, and stood up, stepping to the windows nearby. He turned his head toward me and said, "The subject of Jesus in India has been my hobby during all my adult life." He then turned and faced the windows and the exquisite view of the Himalayan peaks in the distance.

"I don't mean to offend you, but it seems to me that your interest in the subject of Jesus in India is not a hobby, but more like an obsession. Why is that?" I asked.

It was an ironic question, of course, because years later some people would have the same impression about me.

CHAPTER THREE

Mr. Kashmiri continued to stand at the windows, staring out at the distant mountains. I walked over to the windows also and stood a few feet away from his right side, looking at the mountains. It was a spectacular view!

I knew that Mr. Kashmiri had heard my question, so I didn't press him for an answer. Besides, I wasn't in a hurry that morning. We stood there in the pleasant sunlight in a kind of silent reverie for at least two or three minutes.

Finally, Mr. Kashmiri turned toward me, smiled, and said, "I have my reasons." It was a cryptic answer, but that was okay. I didn't intend to intrude on anyone's private matters. But, anyway, I had still had a wonderful, enlightening conversation and I was very thankful that I had met such a remarkable gentleman. I didn't expect that there would ever be any further connection between us about the matter. But there was!

Of incidental note: the Epilogue of the ***Talmud of Jmmanuel*** mentions that ten of the twelve original Israeli tribes had emigrated (for the most part by force) from Israel and settled in what is now Afghanistan, northern Pakistan and India's Kashmir, as well as other realms to the east of Judea. Aziz Kashmiri strongly confirmed the Hebrew heritage of the people of Kashmir in our conversation and in his book. He said that in every aspect of life the Kashmiri people resemble Jews. He also said that the origin of the name Kashmir comes from the Hebrew word "Kashir" meaning one who takes the "Halal" (slaughtered) meat.

He described resemblance of some facial features between Kashmiris and Semitic people, including the nose which sometimes has a prominent "hooked" appearance at top. He also detailed the customs, rituals and many linguistic clues, such as the many Hebrew place names and identical names such as "shaul" meaning "fox" in both languages. He mentioned many other things from his book, such as the distinctive, curved shape of the chopper used by butchers, found nowhere else in India.

In Mr. Kashmiri's book, ***Christ in Kashmir***, on page five it states: "History bears evidence that in 721 B.C., Sargon the Second captured the Kingdom of Israel, and all the Jewish inhabitants were captured and exiled. Most of the tribes came to Iran, Afghanistan, and India and settled down in these lands." Elsewhere in his book, there is considerable evidence that Moses came to Kashmir, the true "land of milk and honey," and is buried there, which adds another dimension of complexity to the mystery. For a wealth of information about the Hebrew connection to Kashmir, I encourage the reader to examine ***Christ in Kashmir.***

Visiting the Tomb of Jesus

After I left Mr. Kashmiri, I later that day went to the tomb of Yuz Asaf on Khanyar Street in the Rozabal section of Srinagar. I entered the ancient building which protects the tomb and found myself alone with my thoughts. I put some money into a collection box for the upkeep of the tomb. I knelt down on the stone floor and after inward reflection, I put my hand on the stone sarcophagus. I rested my hand on the cool stone, breathed deeply and simply reflected. From outside, I could hear the sounds of children playing. It was sunset.

Only a couple of hours before, I was reading in Mr. Kashmiri's book that in 1939, the Viceroy of India, Lord Irwin, who was a devout Christian, went to Kashmir to see the tomb for himself. Another famous visitor at the tomb was Sir Francis Younghusband who wrote ***Kashmir.***

Well, I thought, if this really is the tomb of Jesus Christ, to me it was humorously ironic that I was the only human being on the planet right then who happened to be visiting the grave site. And ironically, I intuitively felt that there was a reasonable possibility that this might be exactly the case. The saying that truth is stranger than fiction sometimes finds confirmation in the most seemingly improbable and unexpected ways.

In a thought related to the sense of high irony, I remembered a scene from the movie **"The Ten Commandments."** Prince Moses had decided to go into disguise as a Hebrew slave and work in the mud pits. He saw an elderly slave man who was hit in the stomach with an axe. Moses carried the man out and held him as he died. The dying man said his only regret was that he had not lived to see The Deliverer. He took a long, questioning look at Moses and died. And, of course, Moses was the Deliverer!

4. Journey to Dharamsala, India: Home of Tibetan Refugees

The jewel of experience is purchased at an infinite price.
—William Shakespeare

The reader is forewarned of a side journey in the search about Jesus in India in this book. The next two chapters involve my arduous journeys through India and Nepal, through inhospitable but beautiful mountains – journeys that nearly brought death to my door. You will see, through my adventures from Dharamsala to Kathmandu, what I learned as a traveler in those lands, with very few provisions and a determination to see the natural country in essentially a primitive way. If Jesus did travel through these lands in primitive times, he saw this fabled part of the world (where even the Buddha began his teachings after attaining enlightenment) in a way that must have to some extent resembled some of my own travels on foot, in which at times I walked for what may have added up to hundreds of miles.

However, for those eager only to stick to the main theme about Jesus in India, and who feel a preference to remain with issues of scholarship as opposed to what was learned and experienced through dogged adventure at personal risk, feel at liberty to skip ahead to Chapter 7: Traditions About the Teenage Years of Jesus.

As for me and my travels, after several mind-expanding days in the Srinagar area, I needed to continue my journey through India and Nepal. I boarded a local bus headed through the town of Jammu, bound for another town called Pathankot. From there, I would change buses and head northeasterly into the province of Himachal Pradesh. My destination there would be the Tibetan refugee community at Dharamsala (sometimes spelled Dharamshala or Daramsala).

Following the Communist Chinese takeover of Tibet in 1959, His Holiness the 14th Dalai Lama and his entourage fled Tibet and were given sanctuary in India. The Dalai Lama and several thousand other Tibetans live at Dharamsala in the northwestern part of India. The late Thomas Merton, a famous Trappist Monk and author, once visited the Dalai Lama at Dharamsala in 1968. Also, in the Steven Spielberg movie, **"Close Encounters of the Third Kind,"** there is a brief scene which takes place at Dharamsala.

When the bus arrived, I found out that Dharamsala is in three parts. Lower Dharamsala, at the bottom of the mountain, is a mostly Hindu town with a somewhat warm and arid climate. Upper Dharamsala is part-way up the mountain and has a mixture of Hindus and Buddhists. The third and highest settlement on the mountain is called McLeod Ganj, and it is almost entirely Tibetan Buddhists.

McLeod Ganj is in a forest of large, beautiful pine trees. The climate there is cool and pleasant, and the air is filled with the wonderful fragrance of the pine trees. The first Tibetans I saw were those who boarded the bus at upper Dharamsala. They came running to the bus in a group, laughing and smiling, like happy children. Many of them, both men and women, wore beautiful turquoise jewelry.

Most of the women wore traditional Tibetan dresses called "chupas" in wonderful pastel colors with multi-colored aprons. The men wore traditional shirts and pants with tall boots and dark coats tied around their waists. Both sexes often had braided hair. The Tibetans

Tibetan Buddhist Library and Archives

smiled easily and seemed to be genuinely good-natured. Their features reminded me a lot of American Indians.

The bus arrived at McLeod Ganj a little before sunset, as the sunlight filtered through the large pine trees. The village is located high in the Himalayan foothills with a sweeping view of the plains below. The air was cool and filled with a delightful pine fragrance. The central part of the village consisted of two parallel rows of Tibetan-type wood and stone buildings with a wide, stone plaza between them. In the center of the plaza was a large, dome-like "chorten," a Tibetan Buddhist holy place. Two long rows of Tibetan prayer wheels flanked the chorten on either end of the plaza.

A Tibetan Ceremony

As I stepped off the bus and shouldered my Kelty backpack, I heard the beautiful, melodic sound of many Tibetan voices chanting softly in unison. I took a few steps closer to the central plaza and found that perhaps more than one hundred Tibetan adults, men and women,

Tibetan Buddhist prayer wheels at Dharamsala, India

were sitting cross-legged on the stone plaza. Many were spinning small prayer wheels in one hand; all were chanting Tibetan mantras, holy phrases. It was such a magical, enchanting scene that I looked all around, expecting that a movie was being filmed.

But it wasn't. There were no movie cameras, and as far as I could tell, I appeared to be the only Westerner there at the time. I had just been watching one of those delightful slices of real life which a traveler sometimes happens upon. As a result of my Peace Corps training, I was feeling a special sense of respect for other cultures. I discreetly waited quietly under some trees until the devotional meeting ended. Everyone strolled away to dinner, and I found a small hotel called the Kailas Hotel. After leaving my pack in the room, I headed off to find a restaurant.

As I was leaving the hotel desk, I met a young Tibetan monk named Ngotup Tsering. He was from a monastery near Darjeeling (place of the thunderbolt) in northeastern India. He was an assistant to His Holiness the Karmapa.

I invited Ngotup to join me for dinner, and we went to a nearby place called the Blue Tibet. We ordered both Tibetan and Western food. I tried the traditional Tibetan tea which contains lots of yak butter and salt. Not bad, but I think it is an acquired taste! Also, I tried tsampa, a Tibetan staple food which is made from ground barley. It is not bad, either. We had a wide-ranging discussion about events in Tibet, and what might happen in the future. My heart certainly goes out to the wonderful people of Tibet and their brave struggle.

After we paid for our meal, I wished Ngotup farewell and turned in early at the hotel.

The next morning after breakfast, I walked westward through the forest to visit a small chapel I had heard about: the Chapel of St. John in the Wilderness.

The day before I was told that Dharamsala was in times past the unofficial summer capital of India. The British Viceroys who governed India used to escape the stifling summer heat of the plains by spending the summer in the cool mountains of Dharamsala. The chapel I visited is in the midst of many large pine trees, in a beautiful setting. No one else was there at that time. I admired the wonderful stained glass windows and wall plaques with names of "Her Majesty's Ghurka Rifles..." and others.

Later, I visited a Tibetan Buddhist Temple at McLeod Ganj and also looked at the outside of the Dalai Lama's house. A short walk away, I found a group of young Westerners studying the Tibetan language at the Tibetan Library and Archives.

It is a beautiful Tibetan-style building in which the top of each wall slopes inward from the bottom.

I explored a lot of trails in the area, enjoying the mountain scenery. I remember many Tibetans made the polite gesture of sticking out their tongues, which means there are no lies in their mouths. Once, I met a cobra on one of the lower trails. I stood still and let him cross the trail!

Mt. Thamserku, Nepal, en route to Everest Base Camp

New Delhi

My next destination was New Delhi, the capital of India. When the bus arrived, I boarded a three-wheeled scooter taxi after negotiating a fare and was headed for a low-priced hotel in the area called Connaught Circus. The name Circus comes from a series of circular-shaped rows of buildings in that newer part of New Delhi. I checked into the small hotel, which was owned by a lady from the province of Goa, India, named Mrs. Lorenzo. Goa was settled by the Portuguese and many of the Indian people there have Portuguese names.

After that, I walked to the train station to buy a ticket to Agra and ultimately to Varanasi (which, as I indicated previously, westerners have long known as Benares). There was some excitement in the station, because a silvery-disk type of UFO had been seen hovering near the station only a few hours before. From what people told me, a lot of people saw the saucer-shaped craft before it darted away at high speed. Many people were still looking upward, wondering if it might return. I believed them and wished I had seen it also.

Later, I visited the old Astronomical Observatory, a set of open-air structures that includes a famous pillar of solid iron which, mysteriously, never rusts. I looked at it, touched it and marveled.

Next, I was on my way to the Nepal Embassy to apply for a tourist visa to visit Nepal. Back in Afghanistan, I had gotten the visas to visit Pakistan and India, but not to go to Nepal.

An amusing scam attempt happened near the Nepal Embassy. An Indian man carrying a woman rushed up to me, acting excited. The woman was moaning and the man said something like: "Sahib, wife very sick! Please give money for hospital!"

I believed them, but I needed to change some travelers cheques into rupees. I apparently spoke too quickly for them to understand, as I dashed away to find a bank. After a few steps, I looked back over my shoulder and saw both of them casually walking away, shrugging their shoulders and chatting. As if to say, "Oh well, he didn't fall for it." I learned to be careful!

Some Advice for Travelers

A few pieces of advice for savvy travelers: many young people use a leather pouch on a strap with the strap going over one shoulder, letting the pouch rest on one side under an arm. This can be a good way to carry your passport, travelers cheques, airline tickets and other valuables.

An even better way is to wear the pouch underneath one's shirt or blouse. A regular wallet or purse can be used to carry a limited amount of cash for daily expenses. Another good system is to use a money belt, which is large enough to hold a passport and other valuables. The money belt should be worn under one's clothing.

Of course, it is always best to go to a secure place such as a hotel room or restroom in order to get something out of the pouch or money belt. In some countries, changing money at places other than banks can bring a much better exchange rate. In some countries it can also be very illegal. Find out what the laws are first. Whether it is legal or illegal, a good rule of thumb is to never change money with a stranger on foot.

Lots of scams involve a very fast and sneaky switching of money. For example, a stranger may approach you on a street and ask if you would like to change American dollars into the local currency, offering you a good rate. He may already have a crisp one dollar bill curled up in his left hand.

Let's say you hand him a one hundred dollar bill and he holds it up to the sunlight to examine it. Suddenly, he looks behind you, says "Police coming. Take your money and go!"

He quickly hands you a curled-up piece of paper money and disappears into the crowd. Later, you examine the money and find it is a one dollar bill. This story never happened to me, but I have heard it from others.

The moral from that story is simply: if you change money at a place other than a bank, do so at a store or place of business. A person on foot in a street or bazaar is highly mobile and can run away; a store owner is basically in a fixed location and is likely to deal honestly.

Putting Your Back to a Wall

Some more tips: if you are eating alone in a restaurant, choose a table at which you can have your back to a wall. In some countries, robbers work in pairs; one can approach you from behind, wrapping his arms completely around you and holding your arms pinned to your sides. Meanwhile, the second robber quickly takes valuables from pockets. Then they knock you down to the floor and both run. If your back is to a wall, they will probably choose easier prey.

My visa for Nepal was ready the next morning. I took an interesting mini-tour of New Delhi for a couple of hours with a Canadian young lady named Michele I had met at the hotel. We went in a taxi to the Parliament buildings and walked for a while outside, among the beautifully landscaped gardens. I noticed the Gurkha guards stationed at various entrances into the buildings. The Gurkhas are a particular tribe from Nepal who have distinguished themselves as outstanding soldiers for hundreds of years. They carry a very large, distinctive knife called a "kukri." In Nepal you will see a lot of them.

Michele told me that she wanted to visit the zoo that afternoon. I happily agreed to go with her because I love animals also. We first went to lunch at a pleasant, air-conditioned restaurant near Connaught Circus. At a nearby table, a group of ladies who appeared to be from different parts of India were having a conversation in English. The national language, Hindi, is spoken mostly in the northern half of India. So sometimes English is the most practical common language for a conversation.

Michele and I arrived at the zoo and strolled the walkways. We were impressed by the kindness shown by the keepers of the animals.

Michele asked me after a while if I had ever been married. I told her I had been close to marriage a couple of times, but travel had interfered. Or we had different goals. I had had a lot of different lady friends through the years, but my extensive travels and my interests that were out of the mainstream had gotten in the way.

Michele told how she had been engaged to a controlling-type of man in Canada and broke things off because she felt as if she were suffocating. Traveling all over the world had been important to her, also. She had to catch a flight the next morning to Athens, where she would be meeting friends and they would travel around Europe together. I smiled at her and wished her a wonderful trip.

The next morning I went with Michele to the New Delhi Airport. We had tea together and visited for a while. We talked about how it seemed sometimes there are too many farewells in life. A hush came over the people in that area, and we turned to see a European woman in a fur coat walking by. The Indian people were all staring at her, and she was obviously uncomfortable. I heard one Indian man seriously ask another if perhaps she had killed the animals herself.

The call came for Michele's flight and we walked together. We kissed and waved goodbye, and she was gone. I watched her plane depart and took a taxi back to the hotel. I finished packing and was soon at the train station, boarding the train for Agra, the city where the Taj Mahal is located. I was in an air-conditioned section of the train. The October days were still pretty hot and humid. The great panorama of the Indian landscape glided past. I wondered if the fabled Taj Mahal would live up to its reputation.

5. At the Taj Mahal and Beyond: A Dream in White Marble

> *Some marvels can only be appreciated fully when seen up close and with one's own eyes*
> —Anonymous

After about two and a half hours, the train pulled into the station at Agra, India. It was getting close to lunch time. Several boys were energetically saying, "Chai! Chai garam! Tea! Hot tea!" as they busily walked along the length of the train, pouring tea into cups made of clay. The great kaleidoscope of humanity in India was streaming in all directions: porters carrying loads on their heads, women in beautiful pastel-colored saris, men wearing robes and turbans of every description, and clothing of every style, Asian and European. Maybe a snake charmer or two, someone with a bear or monkey on a chain. And, of course, all sorts of beggars: some with missing limbs, eyepatches, crutches, some in dancing troupes, clacking spoons and singing. And also, there were pickpockets and thieves on the prowl. Ah yes, train stations in India!

I soon boarded a bicycle rickshaw, and after checking into an inexpensive hotel, I was aboard a three-wheeled scooter taxi and on my way to the Taj Mahal.

Interestingly, I was not able to see the Taj in the distance, as I had expected. I paid the taxi driver and was let off in a parking lot area. From there, I followed several small groups of people walking toward a stone building and wall, which was apparently the entrance. The entry price was very modest. I then walked through the deep shadows and darkness of the entry building to the arched open doorway which faces the Taj Mahal itself and the inner courtyard.

Many people were audibly gasping at that point! In the bright sunlight, the Taj Mahal is glistening, huge, and exquisitely beautiful! The entry portal lines up exactly with the long, reflecting pool, and the entire scene is framed by the lovely, landscaped gardens on either side.

I took a quick picture of the portal with my 35mm camera, and then I walked through and found a vacant area to one side where I could sit in the shade and soak in the view.

The Author at the Taj Mahal, Agra, India

It was a clear, sunny day around the middle of October. The weather was pretty warm, but not too hot. The number of tourists that day was light, not many at all. And, interestingly, most of the tourists I saw were people from other parts of India. The Indian ladies, wearing their traditional saris, walking along the reflecting pool toward the Taj, made a beautiful sight. As I sat taking pictures, one of the caretakers walked nearby and I remarked: "It is marvelous!." He paused and smiled, saying: "No one who comes here is disappointed. It is more wonderful than any picture can convey."

I walked to a white marble platform at about the midway point of the reflecting pool to take a self-portrait with my small tripod. I remembered once seeing a picture of President Eisenhower taken at exactly the same place. That spot, I thought, must be one of the most photographed locations on the planet.

One story I heard from one of the caretakers was that during the India-Pakistan War of 1971, several Pakistani jet fighters were sent on a mission to bomb and destroy the Taj Mahal. The plan was to cripple or reduce the amount of tourism to India, dealing a hard blow to the national morale. Whether a true threat or only a rumor, the Indian military swiftly covered the entire Taj with huge sheets of dark-colored plastic, making it very hard to see The Taj at night from an attacking

jet. They also brought anti-aircraft guns nearby. Fortunately, no attack ever came to the Taj.

Walking close to the white marble walls, I realized for the first time the staggering amount of intricately detailed stone work which had gone into the construction of the Taj Mahal. Built by the Emperor Shah Jahan between 1631 and 1653, it was a memorial tomb for his beloved wife, Arjumand, better known as Mumtaz Mahal, "Ornament of the Palace." The Taj Mahal was built by more than twenty thousand workmen who labored more than twenty years.

Legend has it that after the completion, some of the most highly skilled stonemasons were blinded by the king's soldiers. Thus, they would never use their skills on a lesser structure.

Mumtaz died after the birth of her 14th child. (Maybe the old king loved her a little too much.)

Inside the Taj Mahal

Inside the Taj, the guide explained to a small group of tourists about the intricacy and details of the fine stone inlays and carvings. He placed a small flashlight against one of the white marble walls and moved it to touch the edge of one of the inlayed flower shapes. About the size of a small coin, the flower lit up to reveal that it was made of perhaps fourteen or sixteen separate pieces of different colored precious and semi-precious stones. Each petal of that flower was a different stone of a different color. And the inside walls and stone partitions had a mind-boggling number of such flowers and other details!

After illuminating several flowers, the guide smiled in the semi-darkness, and raising his hands beside his mouth, he looked upward and said a loud "Om!" It sounded to me like there were at least seven distinct echoes which came, one after the other, from completely different directions. He explained that the echo effect was an intentional part of the building's design. We took turns trying it out. It was novel! I can't remember any other place I've been where the echoes sounded quite like that. One story I heard there was that when Lyndon Johnson was inside the Taj, he let out with a very loud cowboy yell. That must have been wild!

I walked thoughtfully around in the beautifully maintained gardens, looking at the Taj from many angles, and from near and far. The story I had read once was that originally, Shah Jahan had planned to have a second Taj built nearby to be made of black stones. However, before that was begun, his power-hungry son, Aurangzeb, seized the throne and had his own father cast into prison at Agra Fort. Thus, Shah Jahan spent the final years of his life staring out of his prison cell, looking at his marvelous creation, the Taj Mahal.

This story, of course, apparently contradicts the story that Shah Jahan blinded his best craftsman so they couldn't work on other structures that might compete with the glory of the Taj Mahal. He could hardly have used them to construct a black Taj Mahal if they couldn't see. (Such is the frustration of sorting fact from legend; one frequently can't have things both ways.)

At the end of the afternoon, I sat with several other tourists and enjoyed watching a spectacular sunset which bathed the Taj in marvelous orange and pink colors. It was awesome!

I took a lot of pictures and even thought about staying there another day or two. However, I really needed to continue my journey. I knew also that the fall weather in the Himalayas, in Nepal, was becoming ideal for trekking in the mountains. And the colder weather would not be too far off. My trek to Everest Base Camp and the return would take twenty days or more. I was excited to think about it!

A young French lady I had met at the Taj joined me for a chicken curry dinner at a nearby restaurant. After saying farewell, I was soon aboard a three-wheeled scooter taxi to pick up my backpack at the hotel.

At the train station, I pulled out my ticket and boarded the overnight train to Varanasi, which is on the holy Ganges River. It is said that every devout Hindu would like to die in Varanasi to attain immediate release from all karma and the cycle of birth and death.

Somehow, I had imagined that it would be a novel experience to try going third class on at least one of my train trips in India. It would be cheap, and most importantly, I would get lots of "local color" – you know, the "real flavor" of India.

Did I ever! It was a time I will never forget! It turned out that many devout Hindus who are about to die will spend their meager life savings to buy a train ticket to go die in Benares. And they ride third class! That part of the train was jammed full of emaciated, suffering humanity. Many of the sick and elderly lay moaning and coughing on the filthy floors. And the stench was horrible!

Normally, I like people and try to be cheerful, but I was getting nauseous. I took my pack and found a friendly train conductor who was able, for a modest fee, to upgrade my ticket to second class and find me a sleeping compartment. I tipped him well and fell asleep quickly, breathing the sweet air.

The Holy Ganges River

Sometime the next day, the train crossed the Ganges River, going hundreds of yards across an ancient cantilever bridge. The Ganges at that place looked very wide and was composed of various shallow channels, with many sandy gravel bars in between.

The Indian people aboard the train were excited and joyful to see the holy Ganges. Many people, even the poorest, threw handfuls of coins out the windows into the waters. Many were chanting, some were holding their hands upward, many were crying. For most, it must have been the first time to see the fabulous holy river they had heard about all their lives. I felt humbled to be there at that moment.

The Varanasi train station was teeming with sweltering humanity that hot, dusty afternoon in October. As I tried to buy a ticket for the journey the next day to a place called Patna, I was told that train service there was suspended indefinitely because of violent riots in which numerous people had been killed. The riots were about some kind of price increase for cooking oil, someone said.

My original plan was to travel overland by bus, train, truck and so on, all the way to Nepal and back to Afghanistan. From Patna, one can go by bus northward to a place on the Indian border called Raxaul. Some people spend the night there and make arrangements to ride, the next morning, on top of a freighter truck into Nepal via a place called Birganj. Then the truck continues on into Kathmandu, the capital and biggest city in Nepal. I had read and had been told that crossing the border from Raxual to Birganj, there is a really spectacular, awesome view of the Himalayas, especially if you are riding on top of a truck!

I thanked the window clerk at the train station, found a bicycle rickshaw driver and was soon on my way to a small hotel I had read about called the Jai Hind. I soon turned on the air conditioning in the small room, took a shower and put on clean clothes.

Later, I was talking with the helpful desk clerk and decided, under the circumstances, to change my overland plans and jump over the problem area. Namely, to get on an airplane and fly from Benares to Kathmandu. The clerk directed me to a nearby Air India ticket office. Soon, I had a ticket for a flight the next afternoon. I would still get a spectacular view of the Himalayas!

Next, I happened to find the same friendly rickshaw driver I had hired the day before. He was relaxing in the shade near the hotel entrance. We made a deal for a two-hour city tour of Varanasi. Specifically, I wanted to visit the area along the Ganges called the bathing ghats, and I also to go to a place a few miles away called Sarnath.

The Life of the Buddha

Sarnath is the place where Prince Guatama Siddhartha, the Buddha, gave his first public lecture after he achieved enlightenment under the Bodhi Tree. That lecture at Sarnath was at a beautiful place called the Deer Park. Also to be found at the Deer Park is a small museum, which contains a famous stone carving called the Lion Column of King Ashoka. This Lion Column is shown on much of the paper money used in India.

En route to Sarnath, my driver took me to a number of fascinating Buddhist temples. Buddhist organizations from various Asian countries have built temples there because of the historical significance of Sarnath. The temples I visited were mostly empty of people, except for one or two caretaker monks. They smiled at me kindly and nodded, and I returned the gesture. Some of the temples contained beautiful paintings of important scenes from the life of the Buddha.

Some of the paintings showed Siddhartha doing great feats of archery, or playing an ancient game called kabaddi, or riding his white horse, Kantika. Others showed Siddhartha with his wife and infant son – or riding with his charioteer and seeing sick, aged and dead people for the first time. Still others showed him living with a wandering group of ascetics in the forest, or meditating under the Bodhi Tree and finally achieving enlightenment. Years later, I saw the wonderful movie, **"Little Buddha,"** starring Keanu Reeves. The movie tells the story of the Buddha in a very charming and entertaining way.

After leaving a small offering at each temple, my driver and I headed off to the Deer Park. At one point, we came to a little hill and as we went up it, I could see my driver was straining on the pedals. Without saying anything, I hopped out of the rickshaw and walked beside him up the hill. He smiled sheepishly at me, and I smiled back, saying "That's okay – it's kind of warm to be going uphill anyway."

At the Deer Park, I bought my driver a soft drink, and then I went strolling around the beautiful park. Tame deer and peacocks walked among the trees, and at one place, I stopped and sat on the grass in the shade of a tree. Closing my eyes, I used the mantra I had learned a few years before in a Transcendental Meditation course. The energy at the Deer Park felt very good.

Later, I walked inside the museum and took a close look at the Lion Column. King Ashoka was a famous convert to Buddhism, and he ruled a vast Indian Empire in approximately 300 B.C. I remembered that back in Afghanistan, at the Kabul Museum, there is an original stela, or stone pillar, from King Ashoka's time.

An Edict from King Ashoka

The stone pillar bears an inscription in three languages, much like the famous Rosetta Stone from Egypt. The writing is a message from King Ashoka in Sanskrit, Persian, and Aramaic, the language of Jesus. It was interesting to me that Aramaic was one of the three languages used, which would indicate that Aramaic was a language known to many ancient travelers. The stone pillar was one of many border marking stones, placed at the boundaries of Ashoka's vast, ancient India

Empire. The writing is basically a warning and welcome saying that the great King Ashoka will not tolerate evildoers, invading armies or the like, and, that he expects visitors to be on their best behavior, or he may clobber them (or something to that effect). Perhaps, I thought, Jesus himself may have read and touched that very stone.

After leaving Sarnath, my rickshaw driver and I headed back to the hotel. I paid what we had agreed on and gave him a good tip besides. I even gave him an extra shirt which I didn't need. He beamed a big smile, thanked me and headed off to his family. I ate dinner at a nearby restaurant, and I was then joined by a young Australian man from the hotel who produced a small bottle of whiskey. It was a brand from Thailand, which he'd carried with him. We both had a small drink, talked some about Australia, women and world travel. Then I left to turn in early.

My alarm woke me before dawn. I dressed and was soon on my way, walking to the shores of the nearby Ganges River, to a place where boats are for hire. I pressed my palms together and said, "Namaste" to a boatman who crushed out his cigarette, smiled and returned the greeting. We made a deal and were soon on our way to watch the early morning cremations which take place at the burning ghats, beside the Ganges. The ashes are then pushed into the river. The human corpses are wrapped in brightly colored cloth, and workers place them atop stacks of wood. The boatman and I watched from the boat, a stone's throw away. It was a cloudy, somber morning.

Looking back at the experience, I remember that I went there that morning because I had read somewhere that the experience would be "unforgettable and deeply moving."

It was!

Since then, I have not gone to see any other human cremations. Some activities of other cultures are perhaps best left alone. Incidentally, I was carrying my camera at that time and the boatman warned me not to attempt to take any pictures there. We would be in great danger of being killed, he said. I agreed with him. Soon I checked out of the hotel and was aboard a shiny, clean taxi going swiftly to the Varanasi Airport. The driver was playing Beatles music, which was fine with me. At the airport, a bearded, turbaned Sikh gentleman working in Customs smiled and stamped my passport, and I was soon aboard an Air India jet. The destination was Kathmandu!

6. Kathmandu in the Kingdom of Nepal

And the wildest dreams of Kew are the facts of Kathmandu...
—Rudyard Kipling

Flying northward, the jet emerged from the monsoon cloudcover, and in front of us was the sweeping panorama of the Himalayas, the highest mountains on Earth. The seatbelt sign was turned off, and many of us stood up and looked out the windows on both sides of the aircraft. It was a spectacular view! Toward the far right, I even thought I could pick out Mount Everest on the horizon. Coming up below us was the great east-west valley where Kathmandu is located. It was a happy moment in time.

At the Kathmandu airport, the unique, twin-banner red flag of Nepal fluttered in the breeze. The Kingdom of Nepal is a country about the size of Florida. After finding my backpack, I cleared Customs and was soon aboard a taxi, headed for a budget-priced place called The Valley View Hotel.

Riding in the taxi, I certainly got a favorable first impression of Nepal. There were not the teeming masses that you see so often in some towns and cities in India. I could see poor people in Nepal, yes, but somehow things looked neither crowded nor wretched. There was neither trash nor debris. Also, I enjoyed the coolness of the high elevation air, the lush vegetation and the spectacular view of the nearby Himalayas.

Nepal is wonderful!

After checking into the Valley View Hotel, I was soon on my way for a late afternoon walking tour. I went first to the Peace Corps office, which at that time was on Janpath Road. The Americans there were civil but not very friendly. I explained that I was a Peace Corps volunteer in Afghanistan, and they kind of nodded and went back to their paperwork. I looked around at brochures a little while and then left. Somehow, I had thought we might have a friendly conversation, or that they might offer some helpful advice. Individual Peace Corps volunteers may be very helpful to visitors (I know I was), but many Peace Corps staff people, just like United States government bureaucrats, are sometimes less than admirable in their display of warmth to strangers.

I shook the dust off my boots and stepped into a taxi headed for the Swayambu Buddhist Chorten. The sunset was beginning when I arrived, and I joined some Buddhist pilgrims walking around the chorten. Many resident monkeys were playing under the nearby trees. Children were also playing near the monkeys as their parents walked and chanted. I saw several large metal dorje (lightning bolt) symbols around the chorten, and high above were painted the two large eyes of the vigilant Buddha.

The Author standing atop Kala Pattar (18,200 feet) with Nuptse, Lhotse and Mount Everest (the dark, windswept mountain) - 29,035 feet)

Later, I went to eat dinner at a place called The Rose Garden Restaurant. There, I happened to meet three Peace Corps volunteers who were working in Nepal. We got into a lively conversation about the good and bad things about the Peace Corps. They asked about my impressions of Afghanistan, and in turn, I asked them their impressions of Nepal. They had a lot of good insights about the cultures and peoples.

The Gate of the Snow Lions, Kathmandu, Nepal

A Yeti Attack

I explained that I would soon be going on the long walk to the base camp of Mount Everest. It is also called the trek to the Solu-Khumbu region, a walk of about one hundred twenty miles.

They were excited to hear about that and gave me some good advice. Later, one of them pulled out that day's copy of the local English-language newspaper, The Daily Nepal, and pointed out a news story of perhaps five or six paragraphs. The piece was titled, **"Sherpa Woman near Namche Bazaar, Attacked by Yeti."** I knew that a Yeti is also called The Abominable Snowman, the gigantic, eight-foot tall, hair-covered wild man of the Himalayas. The American version, found mostly in the Pacific Northwest, is called Sasquatch by American Indians, or simply Bigfoot.

I took the newspaper and read the story with keen interest. After all, in two weeks or so, I was going to be there! I saw that the story, which appeared on the lower half of the front page, was written as a straight news story. Very matter-of-factly. The story told how a young

Sherpa woman had been sent by her parents to watch the family's small herd of yaks as they grazed on a high mountain slope, not far from the village of Namche Bazaar. A heavy fog clung to the mountain slopes on that chilly, autumn morning. The yaks are large, powerful oxen with long coats of hair, adapted to live only in high mountains.

The young woman was alert, ready to scare off any bears or wolves which might try to bother the yaks. Suddenly, from behind, she heard a deep, menacing grunt, and she turned to see a Yeti striding toward her. The Yeti was a large, powerfully-built male, which appeared to be about eight feet tall and was covered with long, brownish-red hair.

The young Sherpa woman was petrified with fear, unable to move or make a sound. The Yeti was intent on going to the yaks, and as it swiftly walked past her, the Yeti gave her a quick, backhanded blow with one of its arms. The hit had great force, knocking her unconscious and tossing her body ten or fifteen feet backwards. Some time later, she awakened on the ground, shook her head, and peered up to see the huge Yeti nearby, squatting over a large, dead yak. Apparently, the Yeti had killed the yak by grabbing its horns and twisting, breaking its powerful neck—a feat no human can do!

The Yeti was tearing off chunks of meat and eating with loud crunching and smacking sounds. The Sherpa woman watched cautiously, and when the Yeti finished and stood up, she pretended to be dead.

The giant Yeti scratched itself and ambled off into the trees of a nearby valley. The Sherpa woman ran quickly to her family and told what had happened. The authorities came quickly to investigate, and the news spread from there. Interestingly, as I write this, within the last several weeks on The History Channel, there was a program about the Himalayan Yeti, titled **"In Search of History: Abominable Snowman."** The show featured a Sherpa woman named Lhakpa Dolma who was attacked by a Yeti! Perhaps this was the same woman I read about?

Of related interest about Yetis: a thoroughly fascinating true story is told in the book by Slavomir Rawicz, ***The Long Walk***. In it, Polish-born Rawicz tells his amazing story of escaping from a Siberian prisoner-of-war camp. During the latter part of World War Two, Rawicz and six other prisoners escaped and walked four thousand miles to freedom! They walked from north of Lake Baikal, across Siberia and

Mongolia, western China and Tibet. After about one year of walking and incredible hardships, they reached British-held India. On the final day, as they descended the last snowy slope of the Himalayas, they had a clear, daytime sighting of two Yetis below them!

Rawicz is now elderly and living in England.

Preparing for a Trek in the Himalayas

The next morning, I went to The Ministry of Home Affairs in Kathmandu to apply for my Trekking Permit. Basically, it is a formality, and it was ready the following day. Two passport-type photos and a small fee is all that is needed. In the rare event that someone should disappear in the mountains, there would be some record of where they went. I picked up my permit the following day. The route I had indicated would include: Jiri, Lukla, Namche, Thangboche, Everest Base Camp. Object of Journey: Sightseeing.

In a guide book, I had read that it is wise to get a large amount of small change for a mountain trek in Nepal. At that time, the advice was to get at least fifty dollars changed into Nepalese one-rupee paper notes. At that time, the one-rupee notes were worth about ten cents in

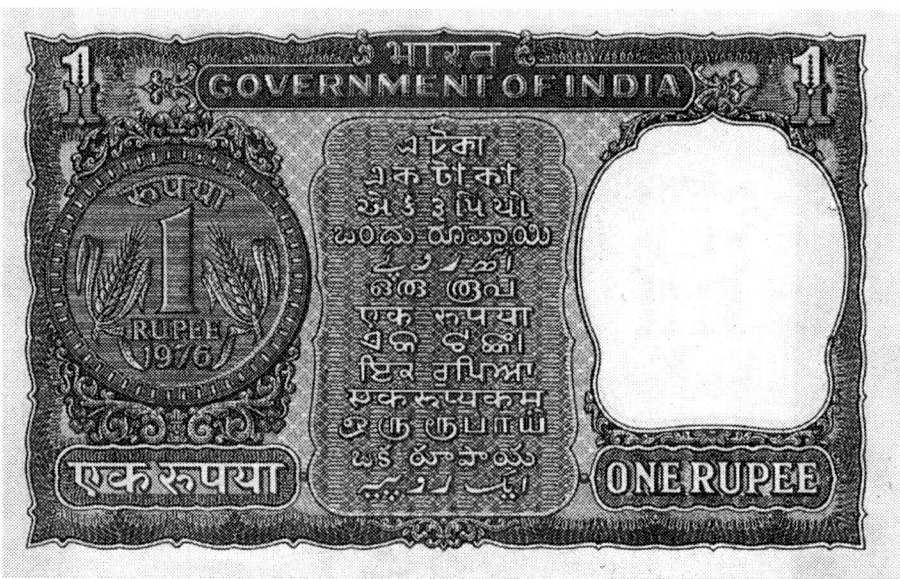

Indian one rupee note showing identification in some of India's major languages, including Hindi, English, Urdu, Bengali, Tamil, Gujerati, Marathi, Telegu, Bihari, Punjabi, Rajasthani, Kanarese and Malayalam

A Nepal one rupee note showing Mt. Ama Dablam

U.S. money. So I headed off in a three-wheeled scooter taxi to several banks, changing ten or twenty dollars at each bank. At the end, I had a stack of Nepalese money which seemed about five or six inches thick!

I wrapped some big rubber bands around it, wrapped it in a big, red bandana and hid it in my backpack.

Next I went to a knife bazaar and shopped around to find a good-quality Kukri, the traditional large, curved knife of Nepal. Many of the serious, adult men of Nepal carry a Kukri in their belt whenever they go on a journey in the mountains. I wasn't looking for trouble, but if something big and hairy knocked me down and started chewing on me, I was damned well going to defend myself. Also, just the sight of a Kukri in the belt of someone who looks unafraid may prevent trouble with a potential thief.

I had the knife sharpened and oiled and put it in my pack. Later, in the mountains, I would carry it on my belt. Also, I bought a sturdy hiking stick, as tall as my shoulder. That would be good for self-defense, too. Later, it may have saved my life.

I went to a variety of grocery stores and camping supply places. I stocked up on some basic supplies, including a large, resealable metal tin of peanut butter. My plan was to mostly eat meals of local food which can be bought along the trail at teahouses, cafes and farmhouses. Instead of carrying a tent, I would arrange to sleep in a farmer's barn or at resthouses. I had been told I would be able to hire a good porter to help me carry half of my things at the beginning of the trek, at the villages called Lamosangu or Dholalghat.

At that time, the wage of ten Nepalese rupees a day, plus food, was considered a decent salary for a porter. At the exchange rate then, incredibly, that came to about one American dollar per day, plus food. At that time also, the average yearly cash income for a rural Nepalese farmer might only be from thirty-five to fifty dollars.

Also in Kathmandu, I stocked up on Kodachrome and Ektachrome film for my 35mm camera. Some of it was previously purchased film (but still good), which trekkers or expeditions had sold before flying out of Kathmandu. Also, I had my well broken-in Vasque hiking boots, which were always comfortable, and my Eddie Bauer goose down KaraKoram "minus twenty degree" sleeping bag. I had used that sleeping bag a lot in Alaska on hunting trips and also when I climbed Mt. McKinley (Denali) only about a year and a half before. The McKinley climb was a twenty-day trip. That sleeping bag had also been with me when I climbed Mt. Kilimanjaro in Tanzania.

A Basic Equipment List

That evening at my room at the Valley View Hotel, I assembled my things and packed my Kelty backpack. Besides my sleeping bag and hiking boots, I had a lightweight goose down jacket, spare shirts, pants, pajamas, socks, bandana, underwear, spare eyeglasses and sunglasses. Also, I had a toothbrush and toothpaste, comb, razor, soap, shampoo, rubber sandals (good to wear in some showers) and toilet paper (it is best to always carry some, and that is an understatement). Also a bath towel and a hand towel. Among my supplies were my camera and film, wristwatch, pen and paper, walking stick, and Swiss Army knife, plus a canteen, drinking mug, bowl and eating utensils. Also, my large Kukri knife, a small first aid kit and a small flashlight with extra batteries and bulb. I also carried some water purification tablets (which, in my case, were not very effective). And a deck of shaved playing cards from a magic store (for card tricks only, not gambling). Finally, I had a lightweight umbrella and a light rain poncho.

Even without a tent, freeze-dried food, a stove, binoculars, pots and pans and some other things, my backpack still felt quite heavy.

The Author's Kelty backpack, which traveled with him twice around the world

I put anything non-essential into a duffel bag and carried it to the hotel's front desk, where I arranged to leave it in a storage room until I returned.

It is one thing to carry a backpack a short distance at an airport or train station, and it is a different thing to carry it on a mountain climb or a long walk in the mountains. I have done plenty of both. My pack still felt quite a bit too heavy (to carry for a hundred twenty miles or more), but I consoled myself with the thought that I would divide the weight with my porter. I wrote a letter home, sipped a little vodka and went to sleep.

Early the next morning after breakfast, I was riding in a local bus, the only Westerner among a group of Nepalese villagers, headed eastward about forty miles or so, to the village of Lamosangu, the beginning point for the one hundred twenty mile walk to Everest Base Camp. A few villagers aboard the bus spoke a little broken English; also, I could speak some simple, basic Hindi which I had learned from a tutor in Afghanistan. Many Nepalese I met spoke some Hindi. I never was a big smoker, but to be sociable, I was carrying two or three packs of Camel Filter cigarettes. As the curious villagers asked me questions, I passed out cigarettes to the nearby adults who wanted them.

Chomolongma: Goddess Mother of the World

For the Nepalese, American cigarettes were a novelty, and we were all smiling and puffing away. Like Clinton would say (though not about tobacco) many years later: "I didn't inhale."

The Nepalese asked me where I was going, and when I told them, "Chomolongma" ("Goddess Mother of the World," the Tibetan name for Everest) their eyes became big. Some asked with hand gestures if I was going to the top? No, I indicated, just to the base. One man asked in Hindi, "Aap ka Sagar Matha jaaega?" "Are you going to Everest?" I told him yes, I was going to Everest. Another man said, "Khumbu Himal?" indicating the Khumbu Glacier which flows from Everest. "Yes," I told them. American? Yes. Alone? Yes.

Everyone puffed silently for a while, deep in thought. None of these villagers, it turned out, had ever walked that far eastward, all the way to the Everest region. They had heard countless stories about the area from Sherpas, porters, and other travelers: fantastic ice peaks, avalanches, rushing rivers of milk-white water, strange tribes and animals, and of course, the Yeti. They looked at me with mixed emotions, as if they thought I was either very brave or very foolish and would be fortunate to return alive.

We talked some more and the villagers all recommended that I begin the trek from Dholalghat, rather than Lamosangu. They said I would have a better chance of finding a good porter there. I took their advice and stayed on the bus for the short distance. The trail from both starting points converges after about one day's walk. From there, it is basically a single dirt footpath all the way to Mt. Everest. At the time I walked it, there was not even one signpost or marker of any kind on the entire route!

Beginning the Trek

At Dholalghat, I retrieved my pack from the top of the bus, strapped my kukri onto my belt, took my walking staff in hand, and I was ready! I said farewell to the villagers and gave each another cigarette. They smiled and nodded goodbye, pointing to the trail I should take. I thanked them and headed off. Right away, the trail went gradually up a hillside. The weather there was fairly warm and sunny that day, and my pack still felt uncomfortably heavy. As I had planned, I

The Author en route to Everest Base Camp, near the Khumbu Glacier

began asking local men who were walking in the same direction if they would like to work as a porter. As I said, that was the advice I was told by several people in Kathmandu: "Oh yes, you can just hire a porter as you go along the trail."

In retrospect, I might have waited in the village, sent out verbal inquiries and interviewed several prospective porters before choosing. However, as it was, things worked out perfectly.

Within ten minutes of walking, a sturdy gentleman in early middle age approached from behind with an empty basket-type pack. He smiled and gave the "Namaste" greeting. He didn't speak any English, and I didn't speak any Nepali, but we both could speak some simple Hindi — perhaps a couple hundred words. Along with hand gestures, we did a pretty good job of communicating. We didn't talk any philosophy, but we got the important ideas across.

His name was Singhbhavadhur. He was a farmer who sometimes worked as a porter, carrying loads for hire. His home was near a small village called Jiri and he lived with his family there. He had just delivered a backpack load for a merchant and was walking back home. His traditional bamboo-basket type of Nepalese backpack was almost empty. The terms I offered sounded good to him: ten rupees a day, and I would pay for his food. We smiled and shook hands. Later, I had to explain that food did not include rice liquor and tobacco. He could buy those himself. We divided things from my pack and set off at a merry pace.

The path from there to the Everest region runs basically east and west; the dozens of river valleys run north and south from the Himalayas in the North. Thus, for most of the trek, you are walking into and out of river valleys. The farther you continue, the more spectacular the scenery. There are all sorts of bridges for the foot traffic across the many streams and rivers. A few, like the bridge across the Dudh Kosi River, which you may reach on the tenth or twelfth day of walking, are modern and sturdy. Sir Edmund Hillary was the main force behind the building of the Dudh Kosi Bridge.

However, many of the bridges on the trek are primitive, even dangerous. Some are not much more than a log about the size of a telephone pole, spanning a torrent of white water. I'm glad I went on the trek, and the advice I would give about bridges is to go slowly and take your time, or you'll end up spinning in rapids.

Singhbhavadhur and I each carried our own umbrella during the trek. There can always be a sudden, unexpected rain shower as clouds sweep into the valleys, and an umbrella is a kind of quick, mini-tent. You can pop it open and squat under it to wait out a short downpour. Or you might have the umbrella covering your head and pack as you walk for hours in a drizzling, misting rain.

Another umbrella use is to occasionally fend off leeches, which in some forested areas will drop from the branches above when humans or animals walk under them. It is a lot more fun to have leeches bounce off an umbrella than to have them on your skin. If a leech does get on your skin, using a cigarette lighter or putting some salt on it will usually get it to release its suction grip.

The first day of walking, we stopped about sunset at a farmhouse and negotiated to buy dinner and to sleep in the hay barn. We had a typical meal of rice, lentils, a few vegetables and some tea with milk and sugar. Later, in the Dudh Kosi river valley, closer to Everest, we were able to buy baked potatoes with butter and salt. That was a welcome change! Also, sometimes we found places where they baked a local sort of flat bread, which was good with the peanut butter I carried. Some people in Nepal, India, and so on, get freaked out by peanut butter! They can't imagine what kind of food it is.

My porter, Singhbhavadhur, near the Dudh Kosi River, Nepal

The trek settled into a regular routine. Every morning, we would get up in the twilight, before the sun came over the mountains. We would get dressed, roll up our sleeping bags and pack. Then a hot cup of tea from a farm kitchen, a piece of bread and fruit, paying for the breakfast, and back onto the trail, walking. We walked basically all day long, every day, from before sunrise until after sunset. We took rest stops whenever either of us needed to, and we stopped sometimes for a tea break, or to eat lunch. I thoroughly enjoyed the scenery and took a lot of pictures.

CHAPTER SIX

Some Close Calls

After a few days of walking, we thought one evening that we might camp out instead of staying in a hay loft. It was close to sunset, and we were in one of what seemed like an endless number of valleys on the trek eastward. But this narrow valley was particularly beautiful and below the footbridge, near the stream, was a broad, sandy area. It looked perfect for camping, and no one else was in the area.

The sky there was clear and starry. We spread out our bedrolls and put up a makeshift tarp as a canopy. After cooking dinner on a fire made from driftwood, we were about to get ready for bed. Then a Sherpa woman came on a trail from the north and crossed the footbridge. She spoke excitedly with my porter and gestured repeatedly northward, to the mountains. Then she walked westward on the main trail, toward higher ground.

Using the only language we both understood, Hindi, Singhbhavadhur explained, pointing to the high mountains to the north, "Bahot, bahot paani vaarhsta!" Meaning, "Lots and lots of rain has fallen!" He indicated the high mountains. "Enja bahot khaternock hay!" Meaning: "Here it is very dangerous!"

I looked at the clear, starry sky above, and also I looked to the far north where thick clouds and fog covered the distant mountains. Reluctantly, I agreed to move on. If the Sherpa woman had not come by, I would have been sound asleep in a few minutes.

We moved camp quickly, crossing the footbridge to the east side. Among the bushes and trees, perhaps fifteen or twenty feet higher than the bridge, we set up our new camp. The mosquitoes were plentiful there, and I went to sleep thinking wistfully about how pleasant it had been in the other location.

A persistent, roaring sound gradually woke me from a deep sleep. It was perhaps one or two A.M. There was a bright moon, illuminating the bushy hillside well. It seemed surreal. The sound was like a rushing train nearby. But there are no trains in Nepal!

Completely baffled, I put on my glasses, stood up and began to walk around barefoot. Then I looked toward the footbridge. The entire floor of the narrow ravine was a raging torrent of churning, white water! The water was only a few inches away from touching the wooden floorboards of the bridge! Our former campsite was under perhaps ten feet or more of raging water. If we had been asleep there, the wall of water would have smashed us against the huge boulders downstream. My porter and I just stared and were silent.

The following day, I began to feel very nauseous. Anything I drank or ate, before long I vomited it up. The convulsions were sometimes like dry heaves. I also had a terrible headache and what felt like a high fever.

My porter and I sometimes had been drinking water directly from the clear, mountain streams. The water looked wonderful, and it was icy cold, but dangerous bacteria or amoebae or some other contaminant must have been in the water. Soon, I had a severe case of amoebic dysentary. I took some basic medicines which I carried in my first aid kit. However, nothing I had seemed to assuage my suffering.

For three days of walking, the illness continued. I kept vomiting up anything and everything: water, hot tea, milk, food. Anything I swallowed, I soon had to vomit. I could barely walk anymore. My porter became very worried, and he told me he had seen people die in my condition. I asked what could be done? We were in a very remote, isolated area, with no hospitals or doctors. Or telephones. I began to wonder if I would die there.

A Tibetan Healer Saves My Life

About then, some villagers approached and asked about my condition. I was lying on the ground, beside the trail, pale and obviously very sick. They felt my feverish brow and told my porter about a nearby Tibetan man who was a healer. They said he was a specialist in traditional, Tibetan-type folk medicine, and that he was a very skilled healer. They said he lived perhaps about two miles north of the main trail, in a forest, near a tiny village called Thodung. They also said that at Thodung there was a small cheese factory, built by the Swiss, which makes yak milk into cheese.

It was nearing sunset, and my porter and I both felt it was an emergency, and that I must get medical help immediately. I was in bad shape and getting worse! We set off on the trail uphill to the north, to Thodung. I had become very dizzy and even more nauseous. I hobbled along but often stumbled and fell down.

Although Singhbhavadhur is a small man, he valiantly tried to help me walk by putting my arm over his shoulders. Soon darkness fell as we struggled uphill through a forest of pine trees. We had seen no

CHAPTER SIX

Sherpas on the Khumbu Glacier, Nepal, approaching Everest Base Camp

one else on the trail. I could barely stand up. Even sitting on the ground, I felt I was about to pass out.

My porter advised me to stay there and rest. He said he would go ahead, find the Tibetan doctor and return with help. I agreed and gave him the flashlight from my pack. He grimly took it and set off. I sat alone in the gathering darkness on the ground. My head was throbbing and spinning with fever, and I was very nauseous. I laid on the ground and didn't think to look at my watch. By now, night had fallen and the forest was completely dark. I went unconscious.

When I woke up, I did not know if it was minutes later or several hours later. A heavy fog filled the dark forest, and the moonlight filtered down, giving an eerie effect. For a startled moment, I wondered if I was already dead. No, not yet. Then for the first time, I seriously considered the possibility of dying there. I prayed and came to peace with the situation, whatever the outcome. Could my porter be lost?

Finally, in the distance, I could hear a voice yelling, "Sahib! Sahib!" I yelled back, hoarsely, and kept yelling. After a few minutes, I was thrilled to see Singhbhavadhur and the Tibetan doctor approaching through the fog. The Tibetan man looked very robust and healthy, perhaps in his thirties, wearing blue jeans and a plaid shirt. Somehow, his wholesome look reminded me of a Tibetan version of John Denver. They got on either side of me and took my arms over their shoulders. I tried to stand and walk.

After ten or fifteen minutes on the trail, we turned off and came to a log cabin type of house with candles and kerosene lamps in the windows. A cheerful fire burned in the fireplace, and numerous children looked out the windows. This was the Tibetan doctor's home. They parked me outside briefly on a wooden bench, while they dashed inside for something. I suddenly had to vomit. Standing, I took a few steps, lost my balance, and fell on the ground. The doctor cleaned me off with a towel and gave me a small cup of a warm liquid to drink right away.

They helped me walk inside the house and sit down for a checkover. Then the doctor gave me pills and more warm liquids, including warm yak milk. Next, I was escorted to a nearby building with several small rooms and helped into a bed. The doctor spoke a little English and told me to sleep. I did so right away.

Mt. Gauri Shankar

In the morning, my headache was mostly gone, and although still weak, I felt much better. The sky had cleared also, and when I opened the door to look outside, I saw Gauri Shankar, a magnificent Himalayan peak nearby in the north. Right then, the Tibetan doctor's wife appeared with a tray of breakfast and steaming hot tea. Soon, the doctor came with a cup of warm liquid medicine and some pills. He examined me and said I would be well enough to travel after two or three days. Also, he remarked that without medical treatment, I probably would have died in one day or so. I agreed heartily with him. He told me that he had seen young foreigners die before from diseases or accidents on the trail to Everest. He said I was lucky.

That afternoon, the doctor brought more medicine and said that if I felt like walking a short distance, just nearby was a Tibetan Buddhist Temple. He said the monks would be chanting and having a ceremony. He told me I would be welcome to visit, and I could ask a blessing for the remainder of my journey. My porter said he wanted to go also, and the doctor gave us each a white scarf to present to the chief monk. The doctor showed us the trail and we headed off through the pine forest.

A cool fog swept in from the north as we walked. It felt great not to have to carry a backpack! We soon came to the Tibetan building where the monks seemed to be expecting us. Inside, the monks sat in

CHAPTER SIX

Mt. Gauri Shankar as seen from Thodung, Nepal, on the trail to Everest Base Camp

rows on the wooden floors, chanting and beating drums. A sweet smelling incense filled the air, and the chief monk sat on a slightly raised platform. No other Westerners were there. My porter gave me the cue to come with him and present the white scarves. In return, the chief monk gave a white scarf to both of us and said a blessing for our journey. We thanked him and left. I was moved by the experience.

During the next day of recuperation, I had asked the doctor about the Swiss-built yak cheese factory at Thodung. He arranged for my porter and me to visit. That afternoon, again in the cool fog, we walked a few minutes and were at the factory. It was small, the size of a medium-sized house, and it looked very clean. The most memorable things for me were several huge, reddish-orange colored metal bowls. They looked like hand-beaten copper and were about four feet in diameter. They were inset into the tables. Large containers of fresh yak milk were poured into the bowls. We tried the yak cheese and it was very tasty!

After three days of healing and rest, the doctor told me I could continue my journey. That morning I paid the balance to the doctor and thanked him for saving my life. My porter and I packed our things and set off again on the trail going eastward. For the rest of the trip, the doctor advised me to only drink water which had been boiled for at least twenty minutes. I followed his advice.

A few days later, another unforgettable event happened. My porter and I had stopped to drink tea one afternoon in a small village along the trail. We were in a drab-looking wooden teahouse with a few local customers. Although I'm normally very careful, I was tired and accidentally dropped my five-inch thick bundle of one-rupee notes as I reached into my backpack. The red bandana around the bundle came completely off, and the huge wad of money, held together by several thick, rubber bands, lay at my feet on the floor.

In American money, it was only about fifty dollars cash, but in rural Nepal, where small farmers might have about thirty-five dollars cash income a year, it was a staggering amount! One man dropped his fork! I looked around, and the few people in the room were all staring, with their mouths open! Quickly, I picked up the bundle, wrapped my bandana around it and put it back in my pack. My porter and I finished swallowing our tea, I paid from my wallet, and we left.

Looking back over our shoulders, we saw three menacing-looking men in dirty clothes staring at us from the doorway. Shortly afterwards, my porter whispered to me that the "three bad men" will follow us and try to kill us to steal the money. In that remote area, there were no police, no telephones. We both had the same idea: it was nearly sunset, we walked very fast and used a leafy branch to obscure our tracks. Then at a place where no one was in sight in either direction, we jumped off the trail into one of the countless, brushy ravines downhill from the trail.

We hid in the brush and trees, and we watched as three men with a kerosene lantern clumsily looked for tracks. We stayed in the ravine that night, had no further trouble, and we resumed our walk the next morning.

A River of Milk

On about the tenth day of walking, we came to the famous "Dudh Kosi" or "River of Milk." The name of the river comes from the fact that glaciers feed the river, and the glacial water carries large amounts of pulverized stone. There is so much white-colored powdered stone in the water that it looks like milk! As I indicated previously, the metal and wood, sturdy footbridge across the Dudh Kosi was sponsored by Sir Edmund Hillary, the first conqueror of Mt. Everest. After crossing the bridge, the trail turns due north and the scenery starts to become fantastic!

Some sections of the trail were like stone steps which descended or ascended for what seemed like incredible distances. Sometimes there were beautiful waterfalls near the trail or just across the valley, which is narrow in places. For the first time we began seeing yaks, the huge, shaggy, high-altitude oxen. Also, we were seeing many more Sherpa porters on the trail, both coming and going. They were usually cheerful and smiling. The trek was becoming more and more interesting as we got closer to Everest.

We passed below the Lukla airstrip, which is situated on the slopes of the eastern side of the valley. Many expeditions and visitors fly into the Lukla airstrip and begin from there. From Lukla, it is only a few hours walk into the big village of Namche Bazaar, and perhaps two days of further walking to Everest Base Camp. My plan was to fly out of Lukla after going to Everest Base Camp. The flights from Lukla go directly to Kathmandu.

Soon after passing near Lukla, my porter and I began meeting Sherpas who said they had just come from Namche Bazaar. That was about the twelfth day of walking. Excitedly, we picked up our pace!

Namche has hotels, of sorts, with hot showers. Also, we had heard that beer was available, among other such things as Coca Cola, ice cream, candy bars, and so forth. My porter and I were having a friendly walking contest!

A dense, cool fog crept down from the mountain heights as we walked uphill for the last stretch into Namche. Several times, large yaks with long, reddish-brown fur were led past by their owners. Finally, we crossed a high footbridge and realized we had arrived at Namche, in the heavy fog. After so many days of walking in remote country, it felt like we had arrived in New York City!

The International Footrest

Right away we located a place to stay which I had heard about, called "The International Footrest," a sort of hotel, which has only one big room instead of private rooms. The big room has wide, wooden stair-step type levels which ascend upwards from the center of the room. In the center of the room is a circular fireplace with a funnel-like copper chimney going straight up into the ceiling. At the level of the highest wooden ledges, there are windows on three sides of the big room. Guests simply unroll their sleeping bag and foam pad and sleep on one of the giant wooden steps. The story was that a visiting French mountain climber who is an architect designed the room. Across a hallway is a kitchen where people can buy food, and there are bathrooms with showers.

Trekkers approaching the Khumbu Glacier en route to Everest Base Camp. White mountain in center is Pumo Ri

After a hot shower, I was ready to walk around a little in the fog. I left my porter at the hotel, talking with a pretty Sherpa girl who worked in the kitchen. It was novel to be in a village of a few hundred people and not see any cars. There are no cars, simply because there are no roads or highways leading into Namche Bazaar. Also, at that time, I didn't see any bicycles, televisions or telephones! And at night, there were no electric lights, only kerosene or gas lanterns or candles. All in all, the people I met seemed happy with their slow-paced, simple way of life. I found a store where I bought a couple of bottles of beer and took them to the hotel.

I awoke at sunrise the next morning and saw through the windows that the sky was now brilliantly clear and sunny. I rolled over in my sleeping bag, where I was sleeping on the top wooden ledge beside a window. As I looked out the window, I gasped with amazement at the dramatic mountain scenery! Some of the spectacular peaks I saw from the window are called the Kwangde Peaks.

After breakfast, my porter Singhbhavadhur told me he was homesick to return to his village of Jiri. I understood completely and paid him his money: a crisp one hundred Rupee note and two ten Rupee notes. He widened his eyes at the sight of so much cash money, thanked me, folded the money carefully and put it into a pouch under his shirt. Then we walked to a nearby shop where I bought him tennis shoes and a pair of socks as a bonus. He smiled, thanked me and placed his palms together in farewell. Then he handed me his own walking stick as a gift, and he was gone.

To Thangboche Monastery and Ama Dablam

Before continuing my trek, I decided to take my camera and look around Namche Bazaar a little, especially since the bright sunlight would be so good for taking pictures. Specifically, I wanted to visit a nearby place called The Everest View Hotel. So I walked just uphill from Namche, passing a place called the Shyangboche air strip.

Some of the visitors to The Everest View Hotel take a flight from Kathmandu to the Shyangboche air strip and depart the same way. The airstrip is at around 14,000 feet elevation. At the time I was there, the story was that only one pilot in Nepal was willing to fly into that airstrip.

I took the trail toward the hotel, and coming around a bend, I was attacked by a large dog. The dog was a German Shepherd and was with a Sherpa woman. She called to stop the dog, but it had no leash or collar. The dog ignored her and was charging at me full tilt, with its fangs bared. Just to my right was an almost sheer drop-off to the huge rocks in the river, far below. I could easily visualize myself going over the edge, with the vicious dog attached to some tender part of my anatomy!

To protect myself, I used my walking stick as a club, and I hit the dog very soundly on top of the head as it flew toward me. That stopped the attack. The dog then responded to the Sherpa woman, and they both walked past me.

Next I heard a galloping horse approaching from the direction of the hotel! To my amazement, an Oriental man dressed like a Mongolian tribesman appeared suddenly, riding a white horse! He stopped a few feet away and looked at me.

Who could this be? And did he speak English?

I put my palms together in front of my chest and said the "Namaste" greeting.

He smiled, did the same and then said in perfect English, "Where are you going?"

I told him I was going to visit The Everest View Hotel.

He replied that he was the manager of the hotel, and he was from Japan. He waved and rode off.

I soon came to the Hotel and was favorably impressed with how it looked. Contrary to some of the publicity I had heard, the Everest View Hotel was a modest and tastefully designed building. It was built by a Japanese company and located high up on the western flank of the Dudh Kosi River Valley. The building is made of beautiful, white stones; it is a one-story building with only ten guest rooms. Each room has a clear view of Mt. Everest. From that angle, the summit of Everest is jutting above the Nuptse-Lhotse Wall, several miles away to the north of the hotel.

I admired the tasteful landscaping around the hotel, also. There were beautiful shrubs, trees and lawns, which give a Zen-like serenity to the setting.

Also, from the hotel there was a spectacular view across the valley eastward to a mountain called Ama Dablam and the majestic Thangboche Monastery below it. "Ama Dablam" means "Mother's Jewel Box." The name comes from a huge, blue ice cornice which juts outward just below the spire-like summit of the mountain. Some people consider Ama Dablam to be the most beautiful mountain in the world. I would give it my vote, also.

I went inside the Everest View Hotel and ordered a cup of hot tea. Sitting in the restaurant area, I relaxed and just soaked in the gorgeous mountain scenery, including Everest.

The lofty, spectacular setting reminded me of Valhalla. I think I was the only young do-it-yourself trekker visiting the hotel right then. I think I looked tan, trim and very outdoorsy – and fully recovered from my illness.

The other guests looked like they had flown into the nearby airstrip and would fly out also. That was fine with me – why shouldn't everyone be able to enjoy seeing the mountains, including those who cannot walk or climb the distance? (I was told there is an oxygen tank in every guest room, in case anyone needs to breathe some pure oxygen.)

It was still only mid-morning, so I walked back to Namche Bazaar, checked out of The International Footrest, and I shouldered my Kelty Pack.

My load was much lighter now than at the beginning of the trek. And somehow, I felt exhilarated to know that in several days I would reach Everest Base Camp, and along the way would be awesome scenery. And not many days after that, I would be flying out of the Lukla airstrip and returning to the comforts of Kathmandu.

Life can be good!

It was early November, and the weather that day was still sunny, cool, and pleasant. That stretch of the trail is marvelous scenery going toward Thangboche Monastery.

I walked steadily, savoring it all and taking plenty of pictures. Later, when I almost reached the monastery, cool clouds of dense fog began sweeping in from the north.

A cold, whipping rain began falling with strong gusts of wind. I quickly placed some devotional objects at the monastery's chorten, as Singhbhavadhur asked me to do. One of the objects was a small, metal trident of Shiva, the Hindu deity often pictured holding a trident. The Hindu trinity consists of Brahma (creator of the universe), Vishnu (sustainer of the worlds) and Shiva (destroyer of worlds). Shiva is much-loved, in spite of the fact that Shiva brings the end to worldly cycles, because in Hinduism, which reveres the cycle of life and all manifest creation, every end is a beginning. Death and destruction comes through Shiva, which brings life and creation anew from Brahma, sustained for ages (or yugas) by Vishnu. Hinduism was never solely an earth-centric philosophy. It challenges us to think in vast spans of time, like the time spans involved in the birth and death of stars and even galaxies. With Buddhism, the same awareness of the infinite march of time is also deeply imbedded, which leads to the high value placed on human patience. If a problem is not solved in a hundred years, then surely it shall be solved in a thousand or a million, which is like a blink of an eye to the deity. So why worry? It also explains the high value placed on meditation, or achieving stillness, for in stillness one is more in tune with the Lord of Creation. Isn't that also what the Bible says? "Be still and know that I am God!"

Inside the Monastery, a monk cheerfully brought me a mug of hot tea, and I sat resting on the wooden floors.

Soon a group of mountain travel trekkers arrived, not in the most cheerful spirits, and they took shelter from the rain. Outside, their porters set up their tents and prepared camp for the evening. I negotiated with the monks to buy a meal and stay in a guest room.

The next morning I left Thangboche Monastery and continued on the trail. Later I crossed another bridge across the Dudh Kosi, and soon I saw the glacial moraines of the Khumbu Glacier.

The Khumbu is the glacier on which Everest Base Camp is located. Sometimes I stopped to buy a cup of tea at some Sherpa's stone hut which had a Cafe sign.

Amazingly, they often build a fire on the dirt floor, with no chimney! This fills the entire hut with very dense smoke. The people lie on the floor, finding clearer air within a few inches of the ground.

I tried it but preferred staying outside.

I camped in a borrowed canvas tent near a stone hut beside the Khumbu glacier. The altitude was probably 16,000 feet or higher. I had slept that high before, in an ice cave at 17,200 feet, when I climbed Mt. McKinley (Denali, 20,320 feet) in Alaska. But it was no picnic. And climbing Kilimanjaro (19,340 feet) had also been a high altitude ascent. Still, it was a fitful, restless night's sleep in the thin, icy air.

To Everest Base Camp and Lukla Airstrip

The next morning I got started at daylight. The sky was clear and at that elevation, it was a very dark blue, almost a purplish color. The trail clung to the left side of the glacier, winding among huge, rounded boulders.

Scattered Sherpas and yaks were carrying supplies for a Polish expedition climbing Lhotse. I was also told that an expedition from Spain had just climbed Everest, and I found a freshly carved tombstone for one of the climbers. The name Dinode Riso was carved into one of the large, white boulders, along with a Christian cross.

After several more hours, I reached a small, turquoise-colored lake at a place called Gorak Shep. A short distance farther, I reached Everest Base Camp. The Polish Expedition had their tents set up there.

I soon walked back to Gorak Shep and the small lake which some people call the Yak Lake. Immediately beside the Yak Lake, to the west, is a small mountain called Kala Pattar, meaning Black Rock. The summit is at about 18,200 feet. The base near the Yak Lake is at about 17,000 feet. It is shaped like a black cinder cone. Many of the famous, classic photographs of Everest are taken from the summit of Kala Pattar.

That's where I went.

It was a fairly easy walk-up to the top of Kala Pattar. The view of Everest and the surrounding peaks is stupendous! Just incredible. And fabulously beautiful!

With the self-timer on my 35mm camera, I took photos of myself with Everest in the background. I stayed up there about one hour, just enjoying the tremendous view and the perfect, sunny clear weather. An amazing place!

A couple days later, I camped for the night at the Lukla airstrip, high on the eastern slope of the Dudh Kosi valley.

The next morning was sunny, calm and cool. Green grass still carpeted the airstrip, but the promise of approaching winter was in the air.

It was almost the middle of November, and I spent a great deal of time thinking about the larger purpose of my expedition and what I was learning and discovering.

Jesus' Travels: A Proposition

I have quite deliberately taken the reader on the journey I took to the less accessible but fabulously beautiful realms of India and its surroundings. I have had great adventures and faced dangers and even death in my travels, on a quest to learn more about the traditions of Jesus' journeys in the same region and to look for evidence and facts while considering both local legend and myth.

Part of my journey was not for scholarly research, but to help gain understanding of what it must mean to be a king of travelers.

I am not a king of travelers myself. Perhaps in chess terms I have become something much more than a pawn of travelers – perhaps a knight or bishop or even a castle / rook? However, the point is, in imagining the missing years of Jesus, all of us have a choice in creating an image of him that goes beyond and transcends the Biblical pages on those years. That is because <u>there are no Biblical pages about those years</u>. There is not even <u>one</u> Biblical page. There is only one Biblical sentence, in Luke: "And Jesus increased in wisdom and stature, and in favor with God and man."

In our imaginations, we can choose to envision that the Jesus of ages twelve to thirty was a stay-at-home future Messiah in a carpentry shop, tending to brothers and sisters and chores for Joseph and Mary, remaining single all the while, when almost all other eligible Jewish boys of thirteen became married. Or we can imagine a Jesus who saw the exotic and fabulous, fabled lands of the East.

If this is the truth about the historical Jesus, who lived and breathed among the people of two millennia ago, he was neither a pawn nor a knight nor bishop nor even a rook/castle of travelers. He was surely the King.

And why should we believe this was so?

This book provides dozens of reasons, but let's grasp first and foremost the fact that among Muslims he is known as Issa, the King of Travelers. He is also called the Prince of Travelers and the Chief of Travelers. And among Hindus, Paramahansa Yogananda states the point of view that during those years Jesus repaid the visit of the three Magi who honored him at his birth. Among the Buddhists at Hemis Monastery in the days of Nicolas Notovitch, the monks also insisted on Jesus having been the King of Travelers, providing Notovitch with an ancient manuscript for him to translate that insisted this was so and offered an exquisite variety of rich detail.

How could three religions with billions of adherents (Islam, Hinduism and Buddhism), all of which accept Jesus as a teacher of wisdom or prophet by names varying from St. Issa to Yuz Asaf – how could they adopt the Prince of Travelers or King of Travelers title for him if it were not so and had no foundation? How could ancient traditions on this develop, if the proposition had no truth or reality at all?

Are we to believe that these ways of describing Jesus were fabricated out of thin air? Why should we conclude such a thing, when Christianity chose to be entirely <u>silent</u> on the issue of how Jesus spent the missing years. Christianity ratified a gaping hole in its New Testament, which in any event was written well after Jesus' lifetime based only upon the surviving and ratified oral traditions?

To me, Christian silence on this question speaks volumes – and this book, this offering, is one of the many volumes that the silence of Christianity spawned.

Also, it appears to me that someone in power a few hundred years after Jesus' lifetime, someone with authority to pick and choose the facts and parts of his life that would make it into the Christian Bible, did not want us to know, did not even offer us evidence or clues to hint at the truth of those eighteen years.

They did not want to offer us a portrait of a Jesus who dwelt also among people of the ancient, eastern religions that pre-dated Christianity – the religions that came to be known as "heathen" or "pagan" beliefs.

All I can say is that devoted members of these "heathen" or "pagan" religions were motivated by their religions and respect for life to save my life many times, and to soothe and comfort me in times of distress, even though I was a Christian "Infidel" from faraway Texas, among strangers.

Even the skeptical reader will hopefully gain an appreciation of why I came to believe that the historical Jesus had likewise journeyed and seen this world, that God the Father fashioned out of nothingness. For in spite of my questioning of some of the tenants of Fundamentalist Christianity, I surely do believe that behind the veils of this world exists God, the ultimate and only creator of our world and all worlds, of people, of all living beings, sentient or spiritual. And I think it much more likely that Jesus furthered his preparations for his ministry by traveling and seeing lands with ancient religions, reaching out to various peoples, rather than being the "village rabbi" who largely confined himself to the walls of a small, provincial carpentry shop, as Christian legend now proclaims.

And so, swept up in both my arduous travels and in the challenge of my search, I traveled on in those inhospitable but beautiful mountains, proceeding step by step as a knight or bishop on the chessboard of travelers, ever mindful of the fact that beyond me and far more perfect than me, there existed a King of Travelers, exactly as Muslims and many Hindus and Buddhists insist upon to this day.

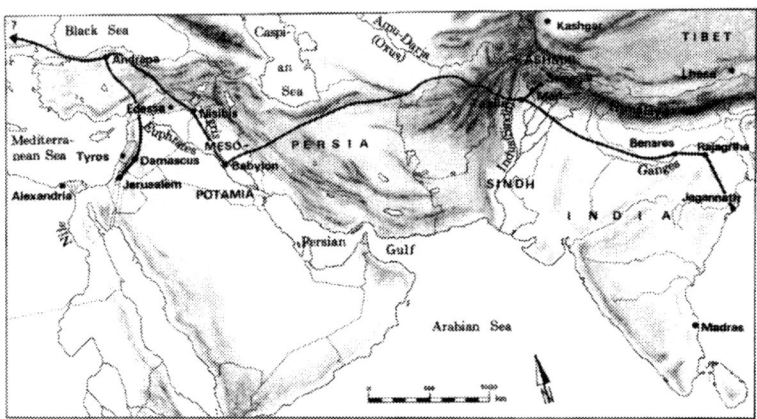

Shaded Map Showing Possible Route of Jesus' Travels

7. Traditions About the Teenage Years of Jesus

All great ideas begin as heresies.
—George Bernard Shaw

At one of the wooden huts at Lukla, I bought a ticket for the flight to Kathmandu. There were a handful of other passengers, mostly trekkers, and some Nepalese people. When I inquired, I was informed that the aircraft was a Pilatus Porter. I remembered seeing some of them in Alaska. They are known for short take-offs and landings. They have a distinctive tail which points straight up.

As we sat waiting for the plane to arrive, I rummaged through my pack, looking for things I didn't really need. Some local children were waiting politely nearby. I took out my large tin of peanut butter, which was still half-full. One of the children expressed interest, and I gave it to him. He smiled, and I gave granola bars to the others. They giggled.

Suddenly, we heard a roaring sound and turned to look down the sloping, grassy airstrip. The Pilatus Porter was flying up from the valley. Some clouds were already sweeping into the valley from the mountains to the north. Many of the children from other huts were racing out to chase grazing yaks from the grassy airstrip.

The plane came up the slope swiftly, pivoted and quickly came to a stop. The engines were throttled but left running. Doors were quickly opened. Passengers rapidly exited; cargo was quickly removed.

Several passengers, including myself, swiftly climbed aboard, and the two pilots readied the controls. The one stewardess checked our seatbelts, and we began takeoff. Some clouds were already approaching the bottom of the runway.

Barreling down the grassy slope at breakneck speed, we gasped as we watched several huge, shaggy yaks scramble out of the plane's path. The children chasing them scattered also, and coming up swiftly was the sheer drop-off at the end of the strip.

The cliff dropped all the way down to the river, far below. A short distance before reaching the drop-off, the aircraft lifted powerfully into the air and soared into the valley. Soon, we rose high above

Namche Bazaar, Nepal

the clouds and headed westward toward Kathmandu. (The clouds can come in and cover the airstrip at any time, making take-off impossible, so we were fortunate in our hasty and unimpeded take-off.)

The great ice peaks of the Himalayas pierced the cloud cover, like glistening jewels, and they made the view incredible! We took pictures and marveled at what we saw. That was the most interesting airplane take-off I have ever experienced! The view of the Himalayan peaks on the way back was unforgettable. Before many days, I would be back in India, learning more about Jesus' lost years.

Pursuing Traditions of Jesus' Journeys

After arriving safely back at Kathmandu, Nepal, in a few days I recovered my strength. For a while, it seemed that I was constantly hungry, even eating five or six times a day. One unusual place I remember going was called Vishnu's Pie and Chai Palace. It was one of several places in Kathmandu which specializes in selling slices of pies or cakes served with hot tea or coffee. In a few days, I felt well again and began my return trip back to Afghanistan, first taking a flight back to Varanasi, India.

At Varanasi, I met with several Hindu scholars and a Buddhist priest. We discussed the traditions and folklore, both written and carried on by the spoken word, that Jesus as a teenager had lived in India. Interestingly, many of the traditions we discussed were focused on the eastern India state of Orissa.

Two locations which were frequently mentioned are the cities of Puri and Cuttack. Interestingly also, the same locations are noted in Levi Dowling's classic book concerning Jesus in India called *The Aquarian Gospel of Jesus the Christ*. As I indicated earlier, Dowling was a Civil War chaplain in the Union Army who claimed that he obtained information ("channeled" information) from the Akashic Records to write his book.

Some traditions state, as in Dowling's book, that a Prince from the eastern India state of Orissa traveled numerous times with his entourage to visit ancient Judea, and such a Prince became the sponsor of young Jesus.

Other traditions, such as those of the Nath Yogis, state that Jesus ran away from home at the age of thirteen and joined a caravan of merchants going to India.

He reportedly was fourteen years old when he arrived in the land of the Five Rivers (Punjab) in northern Sindh. He then went to the Jagannath Temple in Orissa, where he was a student for what may have been a duration of about six years. According to the legend: "He spent six years in Jagannath, Rajagriha, Benares (Varanasi), and other holy cities."

At the Feast of the Passover

The Aquarian Gospel of Jesus the Christ states that during the Feast of the Passover, when Jesus was twelve years old, Prince Ravanna and his entourage were in Jerusalem. When Mary and Joseph missed their son and began looking for him, to their amazement, they found him in a learned conversation with the Jewish High Priests.

One of these priests may have been the famous scholar, Rabbi Hillel. Young Jesus was giving remarkably wise and insightful answers to the Jewish rabbis' most difficult questions about spiritual matters. Prince Ravanna was watching and listening, also.

Prince Ravanna was greatly impressed with young Jesus, and discussed the subject with his royal advisers. Thereafter, Ravanna and his entourage made the journey to Nazareth to meet Joseph, Mary, young Jesus, and the rest of the family.

The proposal which Ravanna made to Joseph and Mary was to become the patron, or sponsor, for young Jesus to travel with his group and become a visiting scholar in India. Jesus was very enthusiastic about the offer and after some days of consideration, Joseph and Mary finally gave their consent.

The royal entourage went by camel caravan to return overland to India. In India, Jesus was accepted as a student at the Jagannath Temple, where he studied the Vedas and the teachings of the Hindu religion. According to the traditions, most of Jesus' teenage years were spent at Cuttack, Puri and Varanasi (Benares). At Varanasi, Jesus studied the Hindu art of healing, including cataract surgery using obsidian blades.

The traditions, as expounded in ***The Aquarian Gospel of Jesus the Christ***, state that Jesus believed in and taught the concept of reincarnation, but not that of transmigration. That is, that human souls incarnate again and again into human bodies, but not into the bodies of animals. Also, Jesus often spoke against the caste system, proclaiming that human equality should be practiced instead. Several times, angry mobs tried to hurt Jesus, but he was always able to escape.

Folklore says that sometime during the teenage years of Jesus, he was notified that his surrogate father, Joseph, had died. This notification was by a letter from his mother, Mary.

Finally, the popularity of Jesus' teachings against the caste system and the Hindu priests reached a critical point. The priests hired a murderer to kill Jesus, but he was warned and escaped from Benares to the north, to Nepal. There, at the city of Kapilavastu, he was welcomed by Buddhist priests to live and study with them.

The Aquarian Gospel of Jesus the Christ further states that Jesus visited Lhasa in Tibet. Levi Dowling states that Jesus studied at a monastery, perhaps at the approximate site of what eventually became the Marbour Monastery. He is said to have studied with the great sage and teacher Meng-ste (also called Mencius by the Greeks). Later, Jesus traveled across Tibet to the Ladakh city of Leh, in what is now northwestern India. There, Jesus spent a number of weeks visiting the area where the Hemis Monastery is now located and where an ancient Buddhist monastery may have preceded it. (Does that explain the portrait of the ancient Israelite young holy man seen by Aziz Kashmiri?) After leaving the region of Hemis (Ladakh), Jesus visited Srinagar and later Lahore, in what is now Pakistan. From there, he joined a caravan traveling westward, toward Israel. And that would be when Christian history, at least the part commencing with Jesus' baptism at the River Jordan by John the Baptist, begins.

Very Ancient Memoirs

Concerning Lhasa and other events, ***The Unknown Life of Jesus Christ*** by Nicolas Notovitch, was first published in 1894 in France, and when translated into English many of the spellings of locations were different from those in use today (i.e., Llasa, Ladak, Himis, etc.) Notovitch says in that book: "In the course of one of my visits to a Buddhist convent, I learned from the chief Lama that there existed very ancient memoirs, treating of the life of Christ and of the nations of the Occident, in the archives of Llasa, and that a few of the larger monasteries possessed copies and translations of these chronicles."

He continues: "During my sojourn in Leh, the capital of Ladak, I visited Himis, a large convent in the outskirts of the city, where I was informed by the Lama that the monastic libraries contained a few copies of the manuscript in question."

Later, he relates: "An unfortunate accident, whereby my leg was fractured, furnished me with a totally unexpected pretext to enter the monastery, where I received excellent care and nursing; and I took advantage of my short stay among these monks to obtain the privilege of seeing the manuscripts relating to Christ. With the aid of my interpreter, who translated from the Thibetan tongue, I carefully transcribed the verses as they were read by the Lama."

Notovitch continues: "Entertaining no doubt of the authenticity of this narrative, written with the utmost precision by Brahmin historians and Buddhists of India and Nepal, my intention was to publish the translation on my return to Europe."

Later, in Rome, when Notovitch showed the manuscript to a cardinal who was close to the Pope, the cardinal replied: "Why should you print this? Nobody will attach much importance to it, and you will create numberless enemies thereby."

The following is a condensed version of the manuscript that was first published in 1894 by Nicolas Notovitch in ***The Unknown Life of Jesus Christ***. The original manuscript he saw at the Hemis Monastery (also spelled Himis) was entitled: ***The Life of Saint Issa, The Best of the Sons of Men***. Presumably written in the aftermath of the crucifixion, the authors (merchants from India who were in Judea at the time of the crucifixion of Christ) would have had no way to know or consider the possibility that Jesus survived the attempted execution on the cross and may have lived to return to India, specifically to Kashmir. Therefore their account assumes, as does the New Testament, that Jesus breathed his last upon the cross.

I

1. The earth has trembled and the heavens have wept, because of the great crime just commited in the land of Israel.

2. For they have put to torture and executed the great just Issa, in whom dwelt the spirit of the world.

3. Which was incarnated in a simple mortal, that men might be benefited and evil thoughts exterminated thereby.

4. And that it might bring back to life of peace, of love and happiness, man degraded by sin, and recall to him the only and indivisible Creator whose mercy is boundless and infinite.

5. This is what is related on this subject by the merchants who have come from Israel.

IV

1. And now the time had come, which the Supreme Judge, in his boundless clemency, had chosen to incarnate himself in a human being.

2. And the Eternal Spirit, which dwelt in a state of complete inertness and supreme beatitude, awakened and detached itself from the Eternal Being for an indefinite period.

3. In order to indicate, in assuming the human form, the means of identifying ourselves with the Divinity and of attaining eternal felicity.

4. And to teach us, by his example, how we may reach a state of moral purity and separate the soul from its gross envelope, that it may attain the perfection necessary to enter the Kingdom of Heaven which is immutable and where eternal happiness reigns.

5. Soon after, a wonderful child was born in the land of Israel; God himself, through the mouth of this child, spoke of the nothingness of the body and of the grandeur of the soul.

6. The parents of this new-born child were poor people, belonging by birth to a family of exalted piety, which disregarded its former worldly greatness to magnify the name of the Creator and thank him for the misfortunes with which he was pleased to try them.

7. To reward them for their perseverance in the path of truth, God blessed the first-born of this family; he chose him as his elect, and sent him forth to raise those that had fallen into evil, and to heal them that suffered.

8. The divine child, to whom was given the name of Issa, commenced even in his most tender years to speak of the one and indivisible God, exhorting the people that had strayed from the path of righteousness to repent and purify themselves of the sins they had committed.

9. People came from all parts to listen and marvel at the words of wisdom that fell from his infant lips; all the Israelites united in proclaiming that the Eternal Spirit dwelt within this child.

10. When Issa had attained the age of thirteen, when an Israelite should take a wife,

11. The house in which his parents dwelt and earned their livelihood in modest labor became a meeting place for the rich and noble, who desired to gain for a son-in-law the young Issa, already celebrated for his edifying discourses in the name of the Almighty.

12. It was then that Issa clandestinely left his father's house, went out of Jerusalem, and, in company with some merchants, traveled toward Sind.

13. That he might perfect himself in the divine word and study the laws of the great Buddhas.

V

1. In the course of his fourteenth year, young Issa, blessed by God, journeyed beyond the Sind and settled among the Aryans in the beloved country of God.

2. The fame of his name spread along the Northern Sindh. When he passed through the country of the five rivers and the Radjipoutan, the worshippers of the God Djaine begged him to remain in their midst.

3. But he left the misguided admirers of Djaine and visited Juggernaut, in the province of Orissa, where the remains of Viassa-Krishna rest, and where he received a joyous welcome from the white priests of Brahma.

4. They taught him to read and understand the Vedas, to heal by prayer, to teach and explain the Holy Scripture, to cast out evil spirits from the body of man and give him back human semblance.

5. He spent six years in Juggernaut, Rajegriha, Benares, and the other holy cities; all loved him, for Issa lived in peace with the Vaisyas and the Soudras, to whom he taught the Holy Scripture.

6. But the Brahmans and the Kshatriyas declared the Great Para-Brahma forbade them to approach those whom he had created from his entrails and from his feet.

7. That the Vaisyas were authorized to listen only to the reading of the Vedas, and that never save on feast days.

8. That the Soudras were not only forbidden to attend the reading of the Vedas, but to gaze upon them even, for their condition was perpetually to serve and act as slaves to the Brahmans, the Kshatriyas, and even to the Vaisyas.

9. "Death alone can free them from servitude," said Para-Brahma. "Leave them, therefore, and worship with us the gods who will show their anger against you if you disobey them."

10. But Issa would not heed them; and going to the Soudras, preached against the Brahmans and the Kshatriyas.

11. He strongly denounced the men who robbed their fellow-beings of their rights as men saying: "God the Father establishes no difference between his children, who are all equally dear to him."

12. Issa denied the divine origin of the Vedas and the Pouranas, declaring to his followers that one law had been given to men to guide them in their actions.

13. "Fear thy God, bow down the knee before Him only, and to Him only must thy offerings be made."

14. Issa denied the Trimourti and the incarnation of Para-Brahma in Vishnou, Siva, and other gods, saying:

15. "The Eternal Judge, the Eternal Spirit, composes the one and indivisible soul of the universe, which alone creates, contains, and animates the whole."

16. "He alone has willed and created, he alone has existed from eternity and will exist without end; he has no equal neither in the heavens nor on this earth."

17. "The Great Creator shares his power with no one, still less with inanimate objects as you have been taught, for he alone possesses supreme power."

18. "He willed it, and the world appeared; by one divine thought, he united the waters and separated them from the dry portion of the globe. He is the cause of the mysterious life of man, in whom he has breathed a part of his being."

VI

1. The white priests and the warriors becoming cognizant of the discourse addressed by Issa to the Soudras, resolved upon his death and sent their servants for this purpose in search of the young prophet.

2. But Issa, warned of this danger by the Soudras, fled in the night from Juggernaut, gained the mountains, and took refuge in the Gothamide Country, the birthplace of the great Buddha Sakya-Mouni, among the people who admired the only and sublime Brahma.

3. Having perfectly learned the Pali tongue, the just Issa applied himself to the study of the sacred rolls of Soutras.

4. Six years later, Issa, whom the Buddha had chosen to spread his holy word, could perfectly explain the sacred rolls.

5. He then left Nepal and the Himalayan Mountains, descended into the valley of Rajipoutan and went westward, preaching to divers people of the supreme perfection of man,

6. And of the good we must do unto others, which is the surest means of quickly merging ourselves in the Eternal Spirit. "He who shall have recovered his primitive purity at death," said Issa, "shall have obtained the forgiveness of his sins, and shall have the right to contemplate the majestic figure of God."

VII

1. The words of Issa spread among the pagans, in the countries through which he traveled, and the inhabitants abandoned their idols.

IX

1. Issa, whom the Creator had chosen to recall the true God to the people that were plunged in depravities, was twenty-nine years of age when he arrived in the land of Israel.

XIV

10. And the disciples of Saint Issa left the land of Israel and went in all directions among the pagans, telling them that they must abandon their gross errors, think of the salvation of their souls, and of the perfect felicity in store for men in the enlightened and immaterial world where, in repose and in all his purity, dwells the great Creator in perfect majesty.

11. Many pagans, their kings and soldiers, listened to these preachers, abandoned their absurd beliefs and deserted their priests and their idols to sing the praises of the all-wise Creator of the universe, the King of kings, whose heart is filled with infinite mercy.

(To read the entire text, the reader is advised to obtain a copy of ***The Unknown Life of Jesus Christ*** by Nicolas Notovitch.)

8. Traditions of Jesus in Lhasa, Kashmir and Tibet

> *And they killed him not, nor did they cause his death on the cross.*
> —The Holy Qu'ran 4:157

According to what the Buddhist monks at the Hemis Monastery told Nicolas Notovitch, the original version of ***The Life of Saint Issa, The Best of the Sons of Men***, was written in Pali language at Lhasa, Tibet. The original scrolls were supposedly written during the first two centuries, A.D. and were kept in a monastery near Lhasa which was affiliated with the Potala Palace of the Dalai Lama. Translations of the scrolls were made in the Tibetan language and sent out to other important monasteries. One of those monasteries was the Hemis Monastery at Leh, Ladakh, in what is now northwestern India.

In Holger Kersten's excellent book, ***Jesus Lived in India*** (Element Books Ltd., 1994), he tells about a surprising number of people who were eyewitnesses of the same documents which Nicolas Notovitch saw in 1887.

Among other eyewitnesses, Swami Abhedananda, of Calcutta, India, undertook a journey himself in 1922 to visit the Hemis Monastery in Leh to verify the facts. The Swami, whose given name was Kaliprasad Chandra (born 1866), had studied at the Oriental Seminary in Calcutta. He later visited England, where he met Max Müller, a noted skeptic of Nicolas Notovitch's story. Muller's negative position was extreme and ultimately unsupportable. He was so interested in debunking Notovitch and the theory of Jesus' travels in India, that he went so far as to claim Notovitch had never even journeyed to Hemis Monastery, when facts (including dental records) proved otherwise.

Swami Abhedananda, while traveling in America, had read Nicolas Notovitch's ***The Unknown Life of Jesus Christ***. Upon returning to India, the Swami went to Leh to try to find out if Max Muller's skepticism was warranted, or if Notovitch had made a true account. In his book, ***Journey into Kashmir and Tibet***, Swami Abhedananda tells on page 119, that he "made enquiries with the lamas and came to know that it was true."

Following the Swami's request to see the information, his book relates:

> *The lama who was acting as our guide took a manuscript from the shelf and showed it to the Swami. He said that it was an exact translation of the original manuscript which was lying in the monastery of Marbour near Lhasa. The original manuscript is in Pali, while the manuscript preserved in Himis (Hemis Monastery) is in Tibetan. It consists of fourteen chapters and two hundred twenty-four couplets (slokas). The Swami got some portion of the manuscript translated with the help of the lama attending on him.*

Tibetan Stone Carvings

Nicholas Roerich and Other Witnesses

Only a few years after Swami Abhedananda's visit, in 1925 the Russian painter and explorer, Nicholas Roerich, who spent many years traveling in central Asia, visited Ladakh. In Roerich's 1929 book, ***Altai-Himalaya, A Travel Diary***, he wrote that he had been told about

Tibetan writings which stated that Jesus had returned from the Himalayas to Judea at the age of twenty-nine.

In Roerich's enquiries among the people of Ladakh, he frequently heard about "the legend of Issa" and the high reverence for Issa. Incidentally, in New York City there is a Nicholas Roerich Museum located at 319 West 107th Street, at Riverside Drive. The director is Daniel Entin, who appears in our film **"Jesus in India"** (www.jesus-in-india-the-movie.com).

Whenever I am visiting New York City, I always make it a point to visit that museum. Roerich's Himalayan paintings are fantastically beautiful! They are extremely poignant and unique works of art (www.roerich.org).

Concerning Roerich, in 1947 the first Prime Minister of India, Jawaharlal Nehru, made the following statement: "When I think of Nicholas Roerich I am astounded at the scope and abundance of his activities and creative genius. A great artist, a great scholar and writer, archaeologist and explorer, he touched and lighted up so many aspects of human endeavor. The very quantity is stupendous—thousands of paintings and each one of them a great work of art. When you look at these paintings, so many of them of the Himalayas, you seem to catch the spirit of these great mountains which have towered over the Indian plain and been our sentinels for ages past. They remind us of so much in our history, our thought, our cultural and spiritual heritage – so much not merely of the India of the past, but of something that is permanent and eternal about India, that we cannot help feeling a great sense of indebtedness to Nicholas Roerich, who has enshrined that spirit in these magnificent canvases."

Another author who wrote about the existence of the Issa manuscripts was Lady Henrietta Merrick. In her 1931 book, ***In the World's Attick***, she wrote: "In Leh is the legend of Christ who is called 'Issa,' and it is said that the monastery at Hemis holds precious documents fifteen hundred years old which tell of the days that he passed in Leh, where he was joyously received and he preached."

A still further witness to the documents was a Swiss traveler, Madame Elisabeth Caspari, who visited Hemis in 1939. She and her group were on a pilgrimage to Mt. Kailas in Tibet. With Mrs. Caspari was Mrs. Clarence Gasque, head of an organization called the World Association of Faith. The librarian of Hemis showed the ancient manuscripts to Mrs. Caspari and said, "These books tell of your Jesus' stay here." Mrs. Caspari briefly held one of the three books in her hands, but the ladies did not express much interest in the writings. Apparently, at some time later, the manuscripts were removed from the monastery. These witnesses are mentioned in Elizabeth Clare Prophet's wonderful book, ***The Lost Years of Jesus***.

In Nelson T. Bruknaer's out-of-print book, ***The Second Life of Jesus Christ***, on page 2 he relates: "After the crucifixion, Jesus lived and taught for many years in Damascus, where he met Saul, who was later called Paul and then St. Paul. Even today three miles from Damascus, a place exists which is named 'Muqam-i-Isa' which is the place where Jesus stayed. Later, together with his mother Mary and his brother Thomas, Jesus traveled over the Silk Road, the great caravan route from the Mediterranean to the Far East. In the historical reports Nisibis is mentioned, which is today called Nusaybin in Turkey. From there the journey continued to Kashan in Persia, today known as Iran, and further to Taxila and Murree, as it is known today, in northern Pakistan. Finally it ended in Kashmir and Ladakh. This first stage of his second life, to the time of entry into Kashmir, extended over some fourteen years. During this time he changed his name to Yuz Asaf (Leader of the Cleansed)."

Also, from page three of Bruknaer's book: "According to the Scriptures and other sources available at Buddhist monasteries of Hemis and Samvas, thirty miles from Lhasa, Jesus was for Buddhism as prophesied around five hundred years before by Buddha Guatama, the awaited successor. It is hinted that Jesus was named 'Bagwa Bodhisattva Avalokitesvara,' 'the white enlightened great merciful All-Seer' – white, because of his lighter skin. He was also referred to as 'he came from a far foreign land'; as 'he was born of a Virgin'; as 'he who spoke in parables' and worked miracles – also as he who rejected the World's riches; preached purity of heart; taught peace and humility and forgiveness of enemies; 'he with the wheel-like marks on hands and feet'—the scars of crucifixion suffered in Palestine decades before."

The Traveling Prophet

Continuing from page three of Bruknaer's book:

> Jesus, Avalokitesvara, it is said, was the teacher of the concept Father-God, Amit-Abha, God the Father, of never ending light. This teaching reformed Buddhism and brought about great changes during the dynasty of the Indian Kusha-

na Kings. The teachings of Jesus became the Teachings of the 'Great Enlightenment' or the 'Great Vehicle' as it is known today throughout the world in Buddhist religion. Before the time of Jesus in Asia, only the teaching of the 'Little Vehicle' had been known in Buddhism, which amounts purely to teaching release from the recurring cycles of reincarnation. As a result of this, many years after the teaching of the 'Father-God' (Amit-Abha) by Jesus, the Fourth Buddhist Council was assembled in an attempt to remove these teachings from Buddhism. But significantly, it is these Teachings which promoted the rise of Buddhism to a world religion. Jesus is associated with great journeys which reached as far as Japan. There exist scripts; they call Jesus the 'Traveling Prophet.' (Messiah also means the same in Arabic). But in every case He returned to Kashmir. In Japan, His teachings of the Father-God, (Amit-Abha) is now called 'Namu Amida Butsu.'

From the famous Persian history **Rauzat-us-Safa** (pp. 130-135) by Mir Muhammad Khawand Shah comes a charming description of Jesus reaching Nasibain, Armenia, which is given briefly in the following:

"Jesus was named the Messiah because he was a great traveler. He wore a woollen scarf on his head, and a woollen cloak on his body. He had a stick in his hand. He used to wander from country to country and city to city. At nightfall he would stay where he was. He ate wild vegetables, drank wild water and traveled on foot. His companions, during one of his travels, once bought a horse for him; he rode the horse one day, but as he could not make any provision for the feeding of the horse, he returned it. Journeying from his country, he arrived at Nasibain, which was at a distance of several hundred miles from his home. With him were a few of his disciples whom he sent into the city to preach. In the city, however, there were current wrong and unfounded rumours about Jesus and his mother. The Governor of the city, therefore, arrested the disciples and then summoned Jesus. Jesus miraculously healed some persons. The King of the territory of Nasibain, therefore, with all his armies and the people, became his followers."

In 1983, Mr. Aziz Kashmiri, the author of **Christ in Kashmir**, attended a convention in Trinidad and was interviewed by the local newspaper. The following are excerpts from that interview, which appeared in The Mirror, Trinidad, Aug. 19, 1983, page 11: Said Mr. Kashmiri, "Jesus did not die on the cross, as is the popular belief, but in fact he had fainted. The evidence which points to this are the Gospels, all of which stated that Jesus was taken down from the cross at the ninth hour, for the other day was Sabbath day, and in those days bodies could not remain on the cross on Sabbath. The histories of those days are a witness that no one died on the cross within such a short time, but normally were left to suffer for many days." (Let the reader recall that Jesus' legs were not broken and he was a strong man in good health). "When Jesus was taken down from the cross, he was actually in a dead faint, and people thought he was dead. Even Pilate, the man who ordered his crucifixion, was surprised that Jesus was already dead ... but he did not know that he was in fact alive."

Marham Isa

Continuing the interview with Aziz Kashmiri in Trinidad:

"What happened afterwards is simple ... he was taken to a cave-like structure where he was rubbed down with Marham Isa, an ointment to heal wounds which is still used up to now. In fact, Marham Isa is called the ointment of Jesus. Anyway, Jesus was rubbed down with this ointment, and was covered with a shroud ... the same shroud making the news these days ... and it was the ointment which caused his form to be imprinted on the shroud.

"When he recovered, some three days later, he was disguised as a gardener (the same gardener Mary saw) as his friends were afraid that Pilate would see him and realize that he was really alive.

"Under this disguise, Jesus fled across the Middle East. When he appeared to the disciples, they thought he was dead, and he showed them his wounds to prove he was alive. He was hungry and was given broiled fish which today is a delicacy among the people of Kashmir.

"Evidence points that Jesus did escape from his enemies, and he was eventually given shelter at another place of which a complete description is given.

"Kashmir is the only place which fits that description. According to the Qur'an, there he lived, carried on his preachings and died at the age of one hundred twenty.

"He was buried in Kashmir, and all evidence points to the tomb in Khanyar Street, which is called the tomb of Nabi (prophet) or the Tomb of Isa (Jesus), as Jesus' final resting place.

"The Qur'an describes the final destination of Jesus Christ as a lofty ground, having meadows and springs, which learned Muslim scholars have claimed is Kashmir."

Later in the interview Mr. Kashmiri also said that he did not want to start any type of controversy with the Christians, but he and the people of Kashmir believe that Jesus did not die on the cross but lived in Kashmir until his death.

"We are not decrying Jesus Christ," says Kashmiri. "In fact we think highly of the Great Prophet. He was a great man, a successful prophet who was given a job to do by God and he completed it – successfully.

"If he really died on the cross as Christians believe, then Jesus did not fulfill the Almighty's wishes." [End of interview]

Traditions from southern India, which I heard about on several occasions, say that the Apostle Thomas lived and taught Christianity for many years in the southern part of India. Many Christians today in the Indian state of Kerala call themselves "Thomas Christians." Tradition also tells about the martyrdom of Thomas, saying that in about the year 72 A.D. near Mylapore, a place close to Madras (now called Chennai), Thomas was killed from behind by a fanatical man with a spear. The tomb of Thomas exists there to this day.

Sign at a Train Station en route to Bangalore, India

Windy Corner, Mt. McKinley, Alaska

9. Unusual Events

> *The Universe may not only be strange;
> it may be stranger than we can imagine.*
> —Albert Einstein

Before I finish writing this book, I would like to share some personal experiences which I think may be interesting and which may possibly stretch your thinking. If we get into the spirit of Albert Einstein's quote, above, then let's explore together some of the aspects of the reality of the world in which we live, which lead us to the conclusion that the universe very well may be stranger than we can imagine.

Whether this helps in a reasonable approach to Biblical mysteries, I leave that conclusion to my readers. And if you must jump ahead, your next strong dose of Jesus in India material comes in Chapter 10: I Learn About the ***Talmud of Jmmanuel.***

However, the following experiences and phenomena are important to me, in that they have influenced my world view and perhaps have made me willing to look for answers to some mysteries in realms that others do not. And so I think you will not be disappointed to stick with me on a jaunt that will ultimately prove to take you somewhere between **"The X-Files"** of real life and my own personal days as a sort of **"Grizzly Man,"** to make two film analogies. After we've taken what ultimately may be a sort of "side journey" together, I will finish with some closing thoughts about Jesus in India and how I view the "big picture."

When I was thirteen years old, my father and I had a UFO sighting along the Colorado River in Texas one night, when we saw a silvery, hovering disk one moonlit winter night. It occurred when we were by ourselves, camping and fishing in a remote area along the Colorado River in Texas. My Dad said, "Let's never tell anyone about this."

Soon after that I was not only reading about UFO's, but also actively looking for them. Often, I would go for walks at night, especially along the edges of the small town where I grew up. Usually, I would carry binoculars, a camera and a flashlight. Sometimes I would see a high-flying light which might move erratically and then dart away at high speed.

At the age of sixteen, I took Driver Education in the summer. Soon after, I got my driver's license. It was great to have the freedom to drive to school, go on hunting trips and to go on dates. Also, as a teen, I liked to sometimes go on clear, starry nights to remote areas to look for UFOs. Gradually, I found some people who did not ridicule UFOs, and some I talked with had seen UFOs up close.

A young lady I met who had lived in a small, south Texas town, described an experience which happened at a drive-in movie theater. She was in a car with several friends, watching the movie. The sky was clear, with a full moon.

She happened to look upward, out of the car window. She was startled to see three silvery disks, hovering silently overhead, with a slight wobbling motion.

She said each disk appeared to be about thirty feet in diameter. Quickly, she pointed the objects out to her friends, who rapidly stepped out of the car and pointed upward. Soon many people were looking and pointing. Someone turned on a flashlight and pointed it at the objects. The disks then, one after the other, shot straight up and out of sight at incredible velocity.

Another friend told a story he had overheard while his father was entertaining a game warden from another county in Central Texas. That part of Texas is also called the Edwards Plateau, or the Hill Country, and it has a large population of the native, whitetail deer. The story from the game warden was that a rancher suspected that one or more poachers were shooting deer at night on his ranch. So the rancher, the game warden and his deputy were 'staking out' the ranch one night.

Silvery-Colored Disks

They were in two vehicles with their headlights turned off, driving around slowly, looking and listening for poachers. It was a starry, moonlit night, and at one point they thought they saw a glint of reflected moonlight from a metallic surface.

The metal object was on a hillside, and the rancher whispered that there should not be any metal objects over there. The trio silently drove closer in the darkness.

A short distance from the object, they heard a strange humming sound. They stopped and watched, when suddenly two silvery-colored disks rose from the ground and hovered at tree-top level. The two saucers each appeared to be twenty feet or more in diameter. After hovering a few seconds, the disks shot out of sight toward the horizon at amazing speed.

The game warden said he had never believed any reports about UFOs, but now, he said, he knew they were real. He finished his story by saying he believed the disks were piloted by visitors from another solar system.

When I was about seventeen, a good friend of mine at high school told me one day confidentially that just the night before he had watched a hovering UFO. He had been asleep, he said, and he woke up because he heard noise from some cattle. He wondered if coyotes were making trouble.

He said he looked out his bedroom window, toward his grandparents' house a few hundred yards away. There, he said, above the corral behind the house, a silvery disk was hovering in the moonlight. At times, the disk was shining down a white-colored spotlight, apparently looking at the cattle in the corral. After several minutes, the disk moved slowly away, out of sight.

My friend and I had done a lot of hunting together – deer hunting, dove hunting and so forth. We knew that area pretty well, even walking around in the dark, with flashlights turned off.

My friend invited me to come out that night and help him look for UFOs, and I accepted. After school, I discussed things with my parents. They both had a tolerant, flexible attitude, especially my Dad, because of the UFO we had seen together and kept secret. I promised to be back before very late, and after dinner I drove to my friend's place.

We each carried a flashlight, turned off, and also we had binoculars and a small camera with a flash. Maybe we were naive, but we had good intentions.

My friend and I walked near the corral where the object had hovered the night before, but we found no trace of it. We then walked a hundred yards or so apart in a long circle around the ranch.

No unusual lights or objects showed up. At one point, for entertainment, we stopped walking, and I made a sound like a wounded rabbit squealing, to call predators. A grey fox trotted up close to investigate. We turned on our lights, and it dashed away. We continued walking, uneventfully.

I told my friend about a time when my father once accidentally called up a mountain lion one night out in west Texas. Dad and I were on a deer hunting trip, and one night, Dad was trying to impress a young couple from a big city by rabbit squealing and calling in a fox or coyote. Instead, a big, bad-tempered mountain lion abruptly showed up! The mountain lion had come running down a mountainside, expecting to steal a wounded rabbit from another predator.

Earlier, Dad had insisted we leave our guns in camp, and we all ran at breakneck speed through a dry ravine to get back to camp! The mountain lion followed behind us, screaming like crazy! Back at camp, with guns in hand, we made sure the lion disappeared for good.

A Really Shocking Experience!

My friend and I had a good laugh at the story and kept on walking. Later, as we got toward the end of the walk, we became separated. I could see the lights of the ranch house, not far away.

Near the ranch house were several corrals. I stopped near one which had a metal fence of some sort. Several prized cattle were inside. Needing to relieve myself, I stood near the metal fence and began to urinate. I stood in the darkness, looking at the beautiful, starry sky and thinking about outer space and other planets.

Very suddenly, as soon as the stream of urine hit the metal fence, I had what felt like a tremendous electrical jolt! Going right through my manhood and all through my body! Just crackling and zapping away! The fence, it turned out, was electrified!!

That was one thing they had never taught me in school. The experience went on for several terrible seconds, because I felt pretty much paralyzed! I don't know if it was my imagination, but it seemed like things were sparking, popping and hissing.

Finally, I made myself fall backwards into the mud, and that broke off the experience. I looked down after a moment and wondered if I had become a neuter gender. But, I was okay. Guys, don't do it!

At the age of nineteen, I talked a friend into going with me on a long drive up to Alaska. My father had always wanted to go to visit Alaska, but he was never able to do so. He had died suddenly from a heart attack when I was nineteen. And so, about three months after his death, I had decided to go.

My friend and I had done our 'homework,' in the sense that we had read books, talked with people who had lived in Alaska and written letters. Driving up the Alaska Highway, the Alcan, was a real adventure at that time. Located in western Canada, the Alcan was unpaved then, 1,523 miles of dirt and gravel, all the way from Dawson Creek, British Columbia, to the Alaska border.

Fighting Forest Fires in Alaska

My friend and I were hired that summer to fight forest fires with the Bureau of Land Management out of Fairbanks. We were called EFF, Emergency Fire Fighters, and we worked with many EFF crews that summer. We learned a lot!

In later summers, I gained even more experience and got to see many parts of Alaska. On one fire, I had a really close call when the wind shifted dangerously, and a friend and I were trapped in dense smoke. By putting our faces to the ground, we found a layer of about six inches of clear air, and we crawled quickly to safety.

The Author at Talkeetna, Alaska, with Mt. McKinley in the background

I was attending The University of Alaska at Fairbanks as a full-time student, and I was fighting forest fires during the summers.

When I was twenty years old, during the summer fire season I was busy as usual. Some heavy rains came in late July, and the fire season seemed about over. So a lot of us took off to do things that August: work on cabins, cut firewood for the winter, get ready for the fall semester and so forth. I planned to go on a big, ten-day hunting trip for moose and caribou. I had arranged with a bush pilot friend to fly me about a hundred miles south of Fairbanks, into the northern foothills of the Alaska Range. It is also called the Wood River country.

My regular hunting friends were all busy with other activities, so I just decided to go hunting by myself. Besides, I thought, my bush pilot friend is very reliable, and he promised to fly over my camp every three days or so, to keep an eye on me. Also, I thought, I would be well-armed, and I had a lot of good equipment and supplies. Grizzly bears, I knew, would be the main danger, but I would be careful and I could certainly defend myself if necessary.

So I got my equipment ready, said my prayers and met my pilot friend. It was a beautiful, cool and crisp fall morning in the early part of August (in interior Alaska, fall does begin in early August). We loaded the equipment into my friend's J-3 airplane and took off from Philips Field in Fairbanks. The J-3 flew at a pleasantly slow speed, perhaps eighty m.p.h. or so, and we flew low, maybe three hundred feet or less above the tundra and forest below. Several times we saw moose grazing, some with strips of velvet hanging from their antlers. A couple of times, we saw old World War Two vintage airplane wrecks rusting away on the tundra.

After perhaps an hour or more, we approached the foothills and had a breathtaking view of the great ice peaks of the Alaska Range. Mountains with names like Deborah, Hayes, Hess, Foraker, and of course, Mt. McKinley (Denali) make a spectacular panorama. Some low clouds were hanging in the valleys of the foothills. We dipped into one valley, skirting the clouds, and we watched a dozen or so wolves running in single file. I was having a great time!

We landed, using the J-3's big rubber tires on a long, flat hilltop, which was free of boulders and had a gravel surface.

We unloaded my gear, Burt smiled and shook my hand, wished me good luck with my hunting, and he said he would fly over my camp in two or three days. If I had gotten something, or if I wanted him to land for any reason, I should spread out a red tarp. Otherwise, he would circle in the plane and fly back home.

Burt climbed into the J-3, waved goodbye, and he took off. I unpacked my orange-colored Eureka tent and assembled the aluminum poles which made the external draw-tight frame. After setting up the tent, I put a few boxes inside to protect them in case of a rain shower.

Then I took my handgun, a Ruger .44 magnum Blackhawk revolver, and I made sure five cylinders were loaded. I rested the hammer on an empty cylinder and put it back in the holster. On my left side was a Bowie knife in its sheath. I picked up my bow, a Bear Kodiak, and my hunting arrows, and I began hunting caribou and moose. I carried the revolver as a precaution, in case I should be attacked by a grizzly bear.

A Big Toklat Grizzly Bear

On the third day, I had still not had any success hunting. I had seen several small herds of caribou and no moose. The caribou were mostly far off, and they seemed wary of wolves. On one cloudy morning, I had stalked through a dense, drizzling fog to approach a small herd of caribou.

I crawled like a wolf and shot an arrow from about forty yards at a group of eight, large caribou bulls. They were standing side-by-side, facing me. The arrow went high, between the horns of one bull. They ran about seventy yards away and stopped. My next arrow went under the chest of one bull, and I watched them run off. I was out of practice with my archery! Too much firefighting.

Walking back to camp for lunch, the wind cleared the clouds away, and as I was in one of the shallow valleys between hills, I heard the familiar drone of Burt's airplane. I couldn't see my camp from the valley, but I could see the plane circle several times. Then I heard the engine cut back, and then came the sound of the plane landing. Something was wrong!

I raced up the side of the narrow valley and was soon at the top. Burt was standing beside his J-3, a couple of hundred yards away, looking for me. I yelled and waved my arms, and he began jogging toward me. I trotted toward him. I could tell he was excited about something and a little out of breath.

"What is it?" I asked.

"Grizzly," he said, catching his breath, "I just saw a big grizzly—a Toklat—walking in a circle around your tent."

A Toklat grizzly bear, we both knew, is a blondish-colored grizzly, one with a lot of long, blond hairs on the back and shoulders. Also, some people have the opinion that Toklats are particularly bad-tempered grizzlies, maybe the worst. And grizzlies are not sweet-natured to begin with.

Burt then described how the bear looked like a very large male. As the bear walked, he said he could see the hide shift back and forth because of the fat underneath. At one point, he said, when he swooped low in the plane, the grizzly stood up on its rear legs, snarled and pawed the air. He said the top of the bear's head looked like it was about ten feet off the ground.

It was scary!

Burt said he had landed to warn me and also to give me the chance, if I wanted, to leave that place and hunt elsewhere.

Then he said that the grizzly might possibly still be in sight nearby, if we looked into the next ravine.

"Sure," I said, "Let's go."

We both checked our weapons. Burt always carried a long-barreled Ruger .44 magnum handgun in the bush. I checked my .44 magnum revolver, also, and then got my .300 Weatherby magnum rifle out of the tent and made sure it was loaded, with a round in the chamber. I put the rifle on safety and then we were ready. We had both agreed only to shoot, if we had to do so in self-defense. That is, if the bear charged us. Otherwise, we would only look.

We trotted a couple hundred yards to where the grizzly had dropped down into the next ravine. Nearing the edge, we began crawling like Indians, to be inconspicuous to anything below.

No animals were in sight.

We looked carefully everywhere, even glancing behind us. Nothing. About then, as we lay on the ground, Burt looked downward between us and whispered, "Here's one of his tracks."

A Huge Track

There, within a foot of our faces, was the biggest grizzly track I had ever seen! It was massively long and wide, and the long claw marks were clearly visible in the soft dirt. I gasped a little and moved a little further away, as though I had gotten too close to a rattlesnake in Texas.

Damn! That was one big bear, and he was still out there, in the big open, free and footloose. Maybe he was watching us, right then, from hiding somewhere. We walked back to the airplane, watching our backtrail.

Burt and I discussed the situation for awhile, and I decided to stay for now. I had become familiar with the hunting area where I was and had scouted adjoining areas. I had made hunting plans, based on the terrain. Moving to a new area, I would have to start over, and I would lose valuable time. And in a new area, there could easily be other grizzlies, just as dangerous. Besides, I thought, the big Toklat grizzly had probably just been ranging through the area and was curious about my camp. Perhaps he was far away by now.

I thanked Burt for his warning. He smiled and said he would fly back over in three days or so. He climbed into his plane, waved farewell and took off toward Fairbanks.

I decided to begin hunting caribou with my rifle instead of my bow. The weather had cleared now, and the caribou were very wary of predators. It would be enough of a challenge to get one with a rifle. It would be helpful to have a supply of caribou meat for the winter.

During the nights now, the aurora borealis, the northern lights, were beginning to appear. Often, they would appear as shimmering, waving curtains of neon-like lime-green and intense yellow, with dashes of bright pink, red or purple. Sometimes looking at the north ern lights was a spiritual experience, deeply awe-inspiring. Also, at night, I could often hear wolves howling in the distance. It was about the second week in August, and the leaves on many trees were turning yellow and orange, fluttering in the wind. The birch trees were among the most colorful and beautiful. The wild roses in the forests had a wonderful smell. All in all, it was a great time to be out in such a glorious wilderness.

The scenery was magnificent the rest of that day, as I ranged over a wide area to the west of camp. The ice peaks of the Alaska Range glistened in the distance like jewels, windswept and awesome. I didn't know at that time that three years later, I would be with Ray Genet and one of his climbing teams, reaching the summit of Mount McKinley! Denali, the highest point in North America! But it happened!

My hunting that day was uneventful but pleasant. I saw a few small, distant herds of caribou and a few cow moose and calves in the valleys. Close to sunset, I arrived back at camp, ready to cook supper and rest. To my astonishment, there was a circle of fresh, huge grizzly tracks around my tent, and they were only about ten feet away from it! It smelled also like the grizzly had urinated somewhere. I almost stepped on some of the tracks, made a sound like "Huuuh?" and then examined them closely, with dead seriousness. I narrowed my eyes a little and touched some of the tracks. It was the same grizzly! The tracks had been made in the last few hours, while I was gone.

Before, when Burt watched the grizzly from his airplane, he said it was about one hundred yards from my tent and walking in a circle around it. Now, after it knew that humans had been here, it had returned even closer. As if to express: "I am not afraid, and I may be back again."

I sat down to think. Certainly, I was an uninvited visitor in the grizzly's domain. Possibly, I might even have been the first human that particular grizzly had ever encountered. It is a huge wilderness, and human visitors are only occasional, here and there, for brief periods.

Grizzly Bear Stories

Well, I didn't know if this grizzly was going to have a hissy fit over me or not. I had heard an abundance of horror stories about what grizzly bears can and have done to people. They can come in the middle of the night. They can rip any tent open in nothing flat. They can stick their huge head in, find your head and crush your skull in their jaws like an eggshell. Or they can rip you to death with their claws, smash your skull with a paw and so forth. They can lie in wait along a trail and then rush you from a few feet away.

If you can put a bullet in the grizzly's head before he reaches you, the attack may be finished. If not, things may become interesting.

I remembered that not many years ago, a big grizzly had killed four adult men in seconds, at one time, near Gunsight Mountain in Alaska. The men, all experienced outdoorsmen, were a hunting guide and three hunters. They had all flown to a remote lake and landed in a plane equipped with pontoons. They were carrying loads of supplies from the shore to their nearby camp when the grizzly charged. Apparently the men were surprised, and either they were not carrying their guns or did not have time to shoot. The big grizzly killed all four men with deadly efficiency.

The bear was never found.

The park ranger-type advice is simply to drop to the ground, go limp and play dead. That is marvelous advice, I'm sure. If you are unarmed and in a national park, that is probably, absolutely the wisest thing to do. But, as they say, the grizzly may never have read that book. In such a case, the grizzly may smell you and then walk calmly away. Or the grizzly may slowly and methodically claw you and bite you to death. Or it might do it quickly. It can be hard to play dead, sometimes, when a big critter is crushing your bones with its jaws.

Some of the feisty, old-time pioneers in Alaska would even stand quickly on a tree stump or boulder and raise their arms, while holding up a spread coat or jacket. The grizzly may judge other creatures by how tall they look and hesitate. The old timers would then make roaring and bellowing noises. Results were varied. If possible, climbing a sturdy tree and going high enough was another thing the old-timers did.

The most recent expert advice I have heard on grizzlies is that there are basically two kinds of grizzly attack situations. The first and most common is a purely defensive situation – for example, a mother grizzly protecting her cubs. Or a bear is surprised and startled. In such situations, the bear may pop its teeth, growl, do a bluff charge and so forth. Playing dead or steering clear may be the best action.

The second attack situation, the experts say, is a predatory attack. For unknown reasons, the grizzly may push things until it meets resistance. Rock throwing and yelling may deter such a bear. Maybe not. If the attack is predatory, playing dead may invite serious injury or death. Consult park rangers and other animal experts before entering grizzly country.

In my situation, if I were attacked, I couldn't rely on help or support from anyone. I knew I could easily bleed to death before my pilot friend would return. I couldn't call 911 or do anything like that. I had no telephone, radio or walkie-talkie.

As I started to prepare dinner, I heard a deep, ominous, growling sound from the nearby brushy ravine. The hairs on the back of my neck stood up. Was it the big grizzly? I looked down from the rim but couldn't see anything in the dense foliage.

Back at camp, after a few minutes, I had the intuitive feeling this particular grizzly might very well come back during the night and kill me as I slept.

And then I decided that I would do something proactive. That is, I would try to take some action and attempt to make things turn out better for everyone. And I knew I might get killed trying, but I also knew I might get killed if I did nothing. After all, damn it, it was my life! And I was not asking anyone else to take a risk. I decided to go talk with the grizzly.

The Athabaskan Indians who were often on crews fighting forest fires had sometimes told me stories about how it can be possible for a human being to talk with animals—and be understood. Some of the Indians believed that bears especially can understand human communication. I always listened with an open mind.

I remembered reading a Sports Afield magazine article written by an Oklahoma Indian who described how Indian hunters would often talk with the spirits of the deer. Before drawing his arrow back, the hunter would silently ask his spirit to talk with the deer's spirit and request permission. The hunter would listen inwardly for the deer's answer.

In the wonderful books **Spiritwalker** and **Medicinemaker** by anthropologist Dr. Hank Wesselman, he describes how human-to-animal communication may take place through means of the "aumakua" or "higher self." He explains that the ancient Hawaiians believed that all large creatures, animal and human, possess an "aumakua."

Talking with a Grizzly Bear

So crazy or not, I decided at least to try talking with the big, Toklat grizzly bear. I made sure my rifle was completely loaded, with a round also in the chamber. I then put my rifle off safety, ready to fire. I checked my pistol, loaded it completely and put the hammer on the safety position. I then looked at my Bowie knife and put it back in the sheath on my left hip, with the strap open. It was late afternoon, nearly sunset. My plan was to look for the grizzly's trail and try to get within talking distance. I would only shoot in self-defense. I would not shoot unless the bear charged me.

I descended into the brushy ravine where I had last seen the bear's tracks. Very soon, I found fresh tracks. Following them, I thought I could smell grizzly scent. After two hundred yards or so, I found what looked like a bedding place in the brush. I had been moving slowly and quietly, being extremely alert—probably the most alert I had ever been in my life. Slowly, I squatted down, looking all around, and I put my right hand on the bedding place. It felt warm. Perhaps, I thought, the grizzly had just gotten up moments before and was only a short distance away, watching and listening.

Since I figured the grizzly could probably hear me, I slowly stood up, looking around carefully. And since I was in the wilderness, with no other humans around, I decided to talk out loud to the bear. I put my rifle in my left hand, extended both arms upward and outward, and I said something like "Hear me, Great Bear! I am a human being and a visitor here. I will only be here a few more days. I am here to hunt caribou and moose. I will only take one. I mean you no harm. If you will not hurt me, I will not hurt you. If you leave me alone, I will leave you alone. But if you want to fight me, then I will fight back, and we both may solve the Great Mystery. Hear my words, Great Bear. Let there be peace between us! I have spoken."

The brushy ravine was silent. Slowly and alertly, I walked back up the slope and returned to my camp. I made a campfire with some dead wood I had collected earlier and cooked dinner. The big grizzly, it turned out, never returned to my campsite or showed up anywhere during the remainder of the hunt. Somehow, I think the Great Bear heard me and we reached an understanding.

A UFO Appears

The next couple of days were pleasant and mostly uneventful, until one evening. I had returned to camp, as usual, after the day's hunting. I was sitting by the campfire and had finished eating dinner. I was drinking a mug of herbal tea and watching the amazing number of stars in the clear, dark sky. I happened to look toward the east and was astonished to see a silent, disk-shaped, hovering object above a hilltop.

From where I was camped on top of an elongated, barren hill, the object was across several ravines to the east, and it was hovering above another barren hilltop. The distance to the object was perhaps between eight hundred yards and one mile. Below the hilltops were the brushy ravines, and nearby to the north was the vast sweep of the forest and marshy lowlands, including the Wood River. Immediately to the south, the hills connected to even higher, treeless hills, and then to the vastness of the ice peaks of the Alaska Range.

The object looked disk-shaped and was glowing with a soft, blue light. The blue color reminded me of the gas flame on a stove. It was hard to estimate size, because there were no trees near the object, but I was estimating that the disk was perhaps thirty to fifty feet in diameter, perhaps larger. It was a quiet, clear night with almost no wind. I strained my ears but could hear no sound from the object. At one point, the object began to shine a beam of white light downward, moving it from side to side. Perhaps it was looking at a herd of caribou below it. Then I thought of my binoculars which were in the tent.

With my binoculars, I could clearly see the disk-shape of the object. It was no helicopter, balloon, blimp or anything else conventional. It looked like a metallic disk which was emitting a soft, blue color. It hovered steadily in the air but sometimes made motions like a boat rocking in the water.

"Well," I thought, "this is one hell of a hunting trip! First, I have problems with a grizzly bear, and next, I see a UFO!"

"This is great," I thought, "just great. I could get abducted by space aliens. Or eaten by a grizzly bear. Or both!"

Then I called to mind the UFO which my father and I had seen when I was about thirteen years old, that winter night in a remote area along the Colorado River in Texas. That was a mysterious experience, yes, but somehow it had always seemed like a positive experience.

On a playful impulse, I reached over and got my flashlight, which had three D-cells. I turned it on and pointed it at the distant UFO, and I said something like, "Okay, guys, here I am if you want to visit."

The white searchlight underneath the object seemed to momentarily point in my direction, and then downward again. A moment later, I reflected about whether these UFO occupants would be a threat – or perhaps friendly?

After watching the object for maybe fifteen or twenty minutes, I became very sleepy and decided to get into my tent and go to bed. Inside, I zipped the tent flaps shut, as always. At least a grizzly trying to get inside would have to make some noise, which hopefully would wake me up. My rifle, loaded and on safety, lay at my left side, pointed toward the entrance. My pistol and Bowie knife lay at my right side. I changed into my sleeping clothes, got into my goose down sleeping bag, and I quickly fell asleep.

Inside-Out Clothing

I woke up suddenly the next morning, with my head beside the tent flaps, which were flapping softly in the breeze. Bright sunlight was outside, and the air was cool and fresh. I glanced at my watch.

It was about eight a.m. I had slept much later than normal. However, I was lying on top of my sleeping bag, not inside. And instead of my feet being beside the tent flaps, my position was reversed, with my head being there instead. If a dangerous animal opens the flaps and starts biting, it is always better to have your feet there than your head. And why were the tent flaps wide open? And then, I noticed that my sleeping clothes, my turtleneck and sweatpants, were turned inside-out!

What was going on?

Back then, I was twenty years old, coming from a Fundamentalist Christian background, and I did not drink any alcoholic beverages, beer, wine or anything. I had never used any drugs or hallucinogens or anything like that. I was not given to sleepwalking, and I was not using any weird medication. Something strange and unusual had happened, I felt. But I had no conscious memory of it!

Why?!

I stepped outside my tent, into the bright sunshine and the cool, pleasant air. The sky was perfectly clear and a beautiful deep blue. I stretched and admired the panoramic, sweeping view in all directions. It was novel to be the only human being in such a vast area.

Something was different! I felt very good, remarkably good. It was hard to articulate, to put into language, but I had the sense that my mind was expanded. It was as though my consciousness was bigger, or better somehow. It was as though I had gotten a spiritual boost somehow. I couldn't explain it, but inwardly it was very real!

Years later, at the right time, I would find strong clues that offered a possible explanation, as unusual and seemingly impossible as it may be, of what may have happened that night. But first, I would have to develop discernment. That is, I would need to develop good judgment and to distinguish between those with whom I could freely discuss unusual events and those with whom I shouldn't.

The rest of the ten-day hunting trip went well, and my friend Burt flew me back to Fairbanks. I shaved and showered, changed clothes, and I spent the next two weeks or so getting ready for the fall semester at the University of Alaska at Fairbanks. Also, to my own great surprise, I was emotionally able finally to make a clean and friendly break with the Fundamentalist Christian church in which I had grown up.

That is, I was able to break free from the oppressive emotional and psychological barriers and leave them behind. I certainly didn't have to talk with anyone, but I politely told the minister and the knotheaded elders that I didn't agree anymore with their condemning, narrow-minded, self-righteous, hellfire-and-damnation ideas. And so I said goodbye and left.

Years later, I was visiting a good friend in Abilene, Texas, a city which is a bastion of Fundamentalist Christianity. A city so conservative it makes your teeth ache. He had been disfellowshipped – that is, kicked out of a church group for attending dances, or some other such hideous thing. He asked how my memories were about that church group and I replied, "Bittersweet. I was happy to be a basically good-hearted young person, trying to do what was right and have fun. And yet I found the religious system to be oppressive and harsh."

Back at Fairbanks, after the hunt, I was getting ready for the fall semester. It happened that an elderly lady named Ada Charlton asked me to make a recording on a cassette, reading from the Bible. Ada liked my voice, she said. She was a retired lady who was a student at the University of Alaska at Fairbanks. I made the recording, and later, to my surprise, Ada gave me a large book as a present.

The book was **The Metaphysical Bible Dictionary from Unity Church of Christianity**. Unity, I found out, is a New Thought type of Church, which includes the optional belief in reincarnation.

Also, in my opinion, they are very positive and not focused on hellfire, guilt, fear, condemning other religions or praising the glorious life of Saul of Tarsus. I became happily involved with the Unity Church.

Hypnosis and UFO Missing Time

Years after the UFO experience that I had on the hunting trip, I began to read about how hypnosis can be used to explore what happened during UFO missing time. In such cases, a person or persons are normally going somewhere at night in a car, when they see a bright light in the sky. Perhaps they talk about the light. The next thing they realize is that they are arriving back home. Mysteriously, perhaps about two hours are missing. For example, if they anticipated getting home about ten P.M., perhaps the time is midnight. They may have no conscious memory of what happened during the missing time, but they usually remember seeing the bright light.

The seminal case of this type was the incident involving Betty and Barney Hill in the mid-1960's, about which many books have been written, beginning with **The Interrupted Journey** up to the recent book concerning the case, entitled **Captured**. The famous New York artist, Budd Hopkins, also wrote several books about the subject of "alien abduction." The first was called ***Missing Time***, and a later book among many he authored was called ***Intruders***, which inspired an NBC mini-series of the same title. My experience by far pre-dated Budd Hopkins books.

Naturally, there are variations of the experience. Some people are walking at night, some are in a boat, some people are in bed, and others have daytime experiences. Among Americans, author David Jacobs estimates are a rock bottom statistic for the number of those experiencing "alien abduction" would be two per cent of the population, including both children and adults. Sometimes this occurs through successive generations of the same family. The real number of "experiencers" may be much higher. That is a lot of people! An ABC News poll showed that sixty-nine per cent of adult Americans believe that intelligent extraterrestrial life exists!

Of course, like anything "paranormal" or seemingly highly unusual, the "missing time" and "alien abduction" experiences have been mercilessly debunked, primarily by a skeptical media and scientific community. The mainstream "establishment" takes the position that we are still looking for the first evidence of any extraterrestrial life — that we don't even have proof of a single celled organism forming outside of earth's delicate biosphere.

Others disagree and insist the human race has been visited by advanced human-like species from elsewhere since before the dawn of civilization, and that even our genetics have been subject to manipulation. Some believe in the intervention in human affairs by advanced "off-world" beings that may have been confused with "angels" during the course of the development of religion. Some even believe that human-alien hybrids have been created.

This is a far cry from Biblical studies, from one point of view. But many writers have pointed out that more than a few Biblical "miracles" and bizarre stories ("There were giants on the earth in those days"… "and the sons of God came unto the daughters of men"… etc.) sound suspiciously like cases of human-extraterrestrial contact.

To explore what had happened in my case, I got in touch with Dr. Leo Sprinkle of Laramie, Wyoming. Dr. Sprinkle is a trained psychologist and is retired from a distinguished teaching career at The University of Wyoming. He and his wife, Marilyn, operate a private clinical practice in Laramie, Wyoming. Dr. Sprinkle is an expert in the use of hypnosis to help people who have had UFO-related experiences with missing time.

Another reason I went to Dr. Sprinkle was because, in my opinion, he has good character and a positive spiritual outlook. Some of my friends in the Edgar Cayce study group had advised that being hypnotized is a serious matter, and it is important to choose a person with a very positive, spiritual consciousness.

Under hypnosis, I returned to the events that happened on the hunting trip many years prioy in Alaska. Leo asked what, if anything, had happened after I went to bed. What I described was that the glowing disk I had seen in the distance earlier was now hovering about thirty or forty yards in front of my tent. It was perhaps twenty feet in the air, and the white searchlight was shining downward. A human-sounding, female voice came telepathically into my head and said, "May we visit you again?"

"Yes," I replied.

Then in my hypnotic regression I visualized three human-like beings coming toward my tent. As they approached, they made walking motions, but appeared to glide about one foot or so above the ground.

They were silhouetted against the white searchlight behind them. They knelt and unzipped the tent flaps, and coming in on their knees, they extended their arms and helped me out of my sleeping bag. Then they kept their arms stretched out, touching on top of my prone body, and they floated me out of the tent toward the hovering craft. We went together, toward the white light, and then together we levitated upward, into the ship.

All of this came to me in the dream-like state of hypnosis. I am not asserting any conviction that it was real, but what follows is the imagery that came to me in the session.

Aboard the UFO

In the hypnotic regression, I found myself on a soft table, which was apparently oval-shaped. The table was gray-colored and was somewhat flexible, like the soft dashboards in some cars. A white light, brilliant but pleasant, was shining from the ceiling. The light was diffused, and I could not see any fixture or bulbs. The sides of the circular room were of a powder-blue color. I had a pleasant feeling, very relaxed, being in the room.

I was on my back on the table, and standing peacefully at my left side were two of the beings. Intuitively, I sensed that they were females. The most striking thing about these beings were their eyes! They have whites and pupils, as we do, but the round pupils are very large. The pupils are circular, about the size of a large coin, such as an American quarter, or even larger. The color of the pupils is a beautiful, deep blue or a vivid purple color. Radiating from the center of the pupils is a starburst pattern, as one might see in some zircons or other birthstones. The whites of the eyes within the skull might be the size of tennis balls.

The beings appeared to me to be a variation of human beings. Perhaps they were even some sort of human hybrids. They had pink skin and mostly hairless heads.

They stood from perhaps four feet, ten inches tall, to perhaps five feet, two inches tall. Their noses and mouths were small. Their ears were also small and close to their heads. They wore what looked like a one-piece type of jumpsuit.

The material looked soft and was a dull-silvery. I didn't see them using their mouths for speaking. I only experienced them communicating using a form of telepathy, between themselves and myself.

They gave greetings to me and said that a long time had elapsed since they saw me before. Somehow, I felt sure they were talking about the time when I was thirteen years old, with my father, camped along the Colorado River in Texas. They said they thought I was doing well on my path. Then they asked permission to take off my turtleneck nightshirt and do some examinations. I told them to go ahead.

Next, a metallic-looking object, about the size and shape of a football, was brought over and positioned above me. The object was not attached to anything, and it floated in the air and remained wherever it was placed. Most of the time, the object hovered about one foot or a little higher above me. My visitors pressed various buttons on the object, and seemed to obtain information from it. Nothing in the entire examination was ever painful.

As the hypnotic regression unfolded, at one point in the examination, I thought to ask my visitors where they had come from. After I gave them the question telepathically, they replied that they did not know what the Earth scientists call their star system or home planet. But it seemed to me that they said that in their own language they call their home planet "Sy-rahs" or "Cyros." They said that periodically they travel to other star systems to do research and observe other intelligent beings. Telepathically asking permission is part of their protocol, they said.

Who can say the extent to which experiences like these, that occur in hypnotic regression, bear any relation to the actual experiences one is trying to access and reconstruct? Some attribute nothing more than fantasy to this type of hypnotic regression imagery. Others believe the subconscious is tapping into blocked memories or screened memories that are real, but to which we have no access in ordinary waking life.

I try not to be attached to these "hypnotic reconstructions" but rather choose to see them as possibilities that lurk in the mind. It's helpful to bring them to the fore, into consciousness. Sometimes they shed some light or knowledge of philosophy or perspective. One doesn't want to lull oneself, however, into a passive acceptance of these experiences simply because one attributes a sort of reality to them in the dream-like hypnotic state.

Of course it's mind-expanding to reflect on them and to feel a certain awe or wonder at the possibilities they suggest. And missing time is an enigma that many people experience. I have never been persuaded by the explanations of the debunkers and skeptics. Sometimes it's best to admit we don't know and take it from there. Ultimately it's the same, to some extent, with the Biblical mysteries I've spent a lifetime exploring. One can take it only so far. We weren't there when those events of long ago happened. Unless, of course, one allows for the possibility of reincarnation. This is very conceivable within the framework of pure Hindu philosophy. However, it is generally ruled out entirely by most Christians, who take the position that we have only one lifetime (to succeed at or screw up), and then our soul goes to heaven or purgatory or hell.

But is that really what Jesus taught, or did those concepts creep in later, through the influence of Saul of Tarsus (St. Paul) and others of influence in the church who followed him. My research suggested to me that the original Christianity as taught by Jesus was probably much closer to eastern thought than the Christianity that predominates today. It appears to have been closer to Hinduism and Buddhism.

And so perhaps some of us, as souls, were "there" in those ancient times and have traces of ancestral memories that help lead us in our spiritual search. (Or perhaps not!)

We look for evidence and collect as much factual material and circumstantial evidence as we can. Ultimately, a sort of leap of faith is still involved, in each of us deciding what we choose to believe.

That's why I offer this book more as a collection of explorations of possibilities and enigmas than as any sort of proof. At a certain point, however, the weight of circumstantial evidence, as in a court of law, does add up to a conclusion of truth. In that regard, the reader must be the judge.

A Spiritual Boost

Returning to the hypnotic regression, I saw that I felt very excited and positive about the entire visitation experience I was having with the "visitors," and I asked if it would be all right for me to tell everyone.

"No, not at this time," they explained. "You lack discernment now, the ability to judge between those you should tell and not tell. Later, with maturity, you will gain that judgment. For now, we must place a barrier of forgetfulness. You will not remember what has happened here, however in the future, when you have discernment, you can find a way to remove the barrier. Then you can remember and tell other people about this time."

In the hypnosis experience, the visitors then asked me if I had any other questions for them. To my amazement, I could not think then of anything else I really needed to ask. I just felt extremely peaceful and had a great sense of well-being. Somehow, at some level, I wished the experience could have gone on for a long time.

Then the visitors asked me if I would like to have a spiritual boost.

"Yes," I replied, "Yes, indeed!"

A few seconds later, another being entered the room. This being, I sensed, was an older male. He projected a very loving, wise and spiritual feeling. He walked around to the end of the oval-shaped table and stood facing the top of my head. He extended his arms toward my head and opened his hands wide. Slowly, he placed both of his hands on top of my head and held still. He stood there in silence for, I think, at least two or three minutes—perhaps longer. The upper part of my head felt an unusual warmth and a tingling sensation, like many small electrical pulses.

I simply tried to relax and be open to whatever the spiritual boost was. Certainly, I could feel that something was happening! Finally, the older male removed his hands from the top of my head, patted me a couple of times on the shoulder and began to walk away.

I sent him a telepathic "Thank you" and he turned, smiled briefly, held a hand up in farewell and left the room. I sent the same message to the two female beings who stood beside the table. They smiled, wished me farewell and said that perhaps they might see me again at some point in the future. One of the females then placed her fingers to my forehead, and I became unconscious.

The next thing I realized was that when I woke up the following morning, as I described earlier, the tent flaps were flapping in the breeze, and there was bright sunlight outside. The strong feelings I had of exhilaration and expanded consciousness seemed to make sense to me. And so did the many peculiar and inexplicable happenings: why my clothing was turned inside-out, my switched sleeping position, being on top of the sleeping bag, the tent flaps being open, sleeping so late and so forth.

None of that was logical given that there was a dangerous bear in the vicinity, and I had taken precautions. There's absolutely no way I would have consciously moved in the tent to sleep with my head against the flaps, or opened the flaps – or for that matter turned my clothes inside out.

Dr. Leo Sprinkle finished the hypnosis session and gave me a tape recording of what had been said. I thanked Leo for his help and paid him for the session. From Leo, I found out about the annual Rocky Mountain UFO Conference, which was held for about four days every June at the University of Wyoming at Laramie. It was always a spiritually-oriented conference and a great event. Then I began attending the International UFO Congress, which is held annually as a week long, usually at the end of February extending into March, in Laughlin, Nevada (www.ufocongress.com)

It was there at that conference, in 2002, that I met Paul Davids, who had come from Los Angeles to speak about his Showtime film, "Roswell," which had a fine cast and had been nominated for a Golden Globe Award as Best TV Motion Picture seven years prior. It featured Martin Sheen, Kyle McLachlan and even country singer Dwight Yoakam in a drama about the 1947 Roswell Incident – the purported UFO crash near Roswell, New Mexico.

Neither of us could have foreseen it then, but three years later, Paul would begin producing and directing *"Jesus in India,"* inspired by this book and based on my research. I am featured prominently in the film, as we embark on a journey across 4,000 miles in India to film and explore further evidence and testimony about Jesus' lost years.

I have written a companion book to this one, about our experience making the film, called **Jesus in India: King of Wisdom – The Making of the Film & New Findings on Jesus' Lost Years**.

Paul Davids on the Ganges River filming a scene for "Jesus in India"

From Afghanistan With Love

Before I close this chapter that encompasses my most unusual experiences, I must mention another of the types of so-called "paranormal phenomena." We'll jump about in time, but it's necessary to convey what happened. First I must mention one of the books I read along the way that made quite an impression on me, called *Jadoo: Mysteries of the Orient* by John Keel. In it, Keel describes visiting remote Tibetan monasteries in the Himalayas, where monks travel outside their bodies. They do that in deep meditation and visit other monasteries, villages and towns. The practice is called "linga sharira" in the Tibetan language.

Upon returning to his body, a monk will describe events he just observed in a distant place. For example, a building burning in a faraway village. The observations were written down and later checked. Often, the information was confirmed!

This phenomenon (a so-called "out-of-body experience") is similar in some respects to what is referred to as "remote viewing" – that is, viewing something taking place at a great distance, by concentrating with closed eyes and conjuring up an image of something one could not possibly know is happening if one were relying only upon the five known senses. Many books and studies have been written detailing CIA and KGB experiments to study this kind of paranormal phenomenon. It was taken so seriously by military agencies, that such experiments were funded and data collected. However, remote viewing doesn't necessarily imply an actual out-of-body experience, because the information could be obtained by some little understood form of telepathy. In any event, I was certainly not aware of the military interest in such phenomena in the days when I served in the Peace Corps.

Before going into the Peace Corps, while I was a student at the University of Alaska at Fairbanks, I was a volunteer with a telephone crisis line. As part of our training, a psychologist from Fairbanks conducted a guided out-of-body session for our group. He had us stretch out on the carpeted floor and slowly take our awareness out of our bodies. Then he guided us to visit remote parts of the world and return. Afterwards, many of us gave vivid descriptions of exotic places, including sights, sounds, smells and so forth. Many of us, including me, wondered if these experiences had been more than sheer imagination, a charge also frequently leveled by skeptics at efforts to reconstruct missing time experiences using hypnosis.

However, this type of "paranormal experience" is not without various types of confirming evidence, which I was to discover personally.

Not long before meeting up with the psychologist from Fairbanks, I had read a very unusual book by Jack London called **The Star Rover**. In that book, a man being held prisoner and put in a straitjacket finds that he is able to make his spirit leave his body. During these "astral projections" he is able to travel through space and also through time.

Suffice it to say that I was intrigued by the book and fascinated by the stories in it – and equally fascinated with the guided out-of-body exploration while I was a student in college.

During my stint in the Peace Corps in Afghanistan, at one point, when I had been there about six months, like many Americans, I became depressed, feeling very unwelcome and unappreciated. After work, I rode my bicycle back home, dodging piles of camel manure and wild traffic, and I just sat in my room for a long time. I looked outside at the garden and felt a terrible, wrenching feeling of homesickness. I wanted to stay long enough to have vacation time and see India, but at times I had an almost overwhelming sadness about being in Afghanistan. Then I thought about the out-of-body experience in Alaska and decided to try to experience that state again as a form of escape from my depression and lengthy separation from home.

I lay down on my Afghan-made bed, called a "chor-poi" ("four legs") and stretched out. I breathed deeply and began to withdraw slowly my consciousness from my body. Finally, I visualized my soul coming out of my body through the "third eye" in my forehead. Then I had the sensation of floating up to the ceiling of the room and looking down at my body resting motionless on the bed below.

Next, in my effort at out-of-body travel, I sensed a part of myself going up through the ceiling and roof and looking down at the house from about fifty feet above. Also, I looked around at the view of Kabul and the Hindu Kush mountains nearby. Then, in this out-of-body experience, I turned westward and was flying faster than a jet airplane, and I visualized going back to my home town of Lampasas in Texas. I saw my home town from the air as I approached in spirit. I had seen it also, in years past, from an airplane, so I knew well what it looked like.

A Surprise Visit

My father had died about four years before, but my mother was still alive. My parents had owned a dry cleaning and laundry business, which my mother still owned and operated.

In "my mind's eye" I located my mother's dry cleaning business from above and swooped down, landing in the parking lot behind the building. I looked around at the cars that were there, observed the trees, green plants and grass. No people were in sight. Then in the out-of-body vision I saw and felt myself entering the rear of the building as I had done before as a child and young person, countless times. I went past the long, humming boiler, glanced at stacks of hanger boxes and came to an open door. There, beyond the boiler room, was the scrub vat room, a place where normally only one employee at a time worked.

The eight or so employees took turns, one at a time, scrubbing dirty clothes in a running water vat. Even though my mother owned the business and enjoyed working the cash register at the front of the establishment, she regularly took a turn at the scrub vat. And it happened that day, as I astrally projected myself there, that I found my mother working at the scrub vat.

I was amused at how vigorously she was scrubbing away and humming a merry song. I concentrated on collecting my energy to speak and say something! I know it sounds impossible to make audible sounds without a physical body being there, but it worked!

From my readings of the works of Yogananda and my foray into Transcendental Meditation, I knew about the concept of prana – the fundamental, free-floating life energy that surrounds us and fills us with every breath. I tried to gather some of that prana and concentrate it in order to say: "Hi, Mom, how are you doing?"

I was watching my mother's back, and at my words, she stood bolt upright, as though startled, and then she dropped the scrub brush.

She whirled around and looked straight at me and around me. By then, I was standing near the large, old safe, which was near the door and among a lot of unclaimed, hanging clothes. My mother was intently looking for me and walking toward me. About then, I felt the pull to leave, as though my energy level would not let me stay longer. I tried to say "Goodbye" and felt myself being pulled out of the building.

Then as the out-of-body vision continued, I went up, high into the air and headed back toward Afghanistan. I had the impression of being connected to my body by a very long, thin silver string that kept my soul attached to my physical body. (How's *that* for a new form of "string theory"?)

Rapidly, I returned to Afghanistan and to my motionless body on the bed. The house was completely dark and silent except for the ticking of a clock on the wall and the soft snoring of my housemate, another young man in the Peace Corps, who slept in another part of the house. I changed into my pajamas, set my alarm clock and fell asleep.

Although I wrote letters about once a week to my mother, I never wrote about the attempt at astral projection. After all, I felt it must have only been an imaginary experience.

At almost the end of the year, after I had spent a year teaching in Afghanistan and traveled in Pakistan, India and Nepal, I was able to visit Texas again. (This was before my assignment in the Peace Corps to depart from Afghanistan to serve in the Fiji Islands in the South Pacific, where I taught for two years.)

Arriving Back in Texas

Arriving back in Texas one cold December evening, I greeted my mother as she met me at the Austin Airport. After getting my baggage, we put it in the car and began driving away from the airport. I was astounded when, on her own initiative, my mother began to describe her experience of the "scrub vat" story—with great enthusiasm! I had never written or told anyone about the "out-of-body experience" or astral projection!

My mother described how, about six months before, she had one day been working alone in the scrub vat room at the cleaners. Suddenly, as she was scrubbing some blue jeans, she heard my voice, loud and clear, coming from behind her. She said she heard something like, "Hi, Mom. How are you doing?"

She said that she was completely surprised because she knew I was on the other side of the world, in Afghanistan or India! Then she thought I must have returned home secretly, as a surprise. From my letters she knew I was not really happy working in Afghanistan. She told me that she searched for me, for a long time, among the unclaimed clothing. She had heard my voice so clearly! I must be hiding somewhere in the room, she thought. Finally, when she had searched everywhere, she sat down and began crying, she said. Some of her employees came in the room then and found her weeping.

I explained to my mother about the "out-of-body experience" I had in Afghanistan and told her the details of what happened. She said she was skeptical about "out-of-body experiences," but she could not come up with an explanation for having heard my voice so clearly.

A sign says that it's the Dalai Lama's 70th Birthday as our film crew arrives in Dharamsala in 2005 to film "Jesus in India" and seek an interview with him. Finally, he agreed to appear in the film.

After 31 years, I am finally reunited with Aziz Kashmirir(and meet his grandson) in Srinagar in 2005, as we film in the war-torn city near the Tomb of Yuz Asaf

Filming "Jesus in India" we had an historic interview with the Shankaracharya, the leader of Hinduism, near the ancient Jagannath Temple in Puri, India. He insists that Jesus spent years in Puri and Kashmir.

Filming at Meenakshi Temple in Madurai, we met with the High Priests who told of Jesus' sojourn in Tibet

In Calcutta, the Filming Team approaches the Boyhood Neighborhood of Paramahansa Yogananda, the author of "Autobiography of a Yogi," who claims the Three Magi were rishis (advanced souls) from India

The Producers of "Jesus in India" traveled by Rickshaw to reach the Golden Temple of the Sikhs

The Founder of ISKCON (International Society for Krishna Consciousness in Bangalore) also claims that young Jesus studied at the Jagannath Temple

The oars of the Dal Lake boatmen in Srinagar, Kashmir (who row "Shikaras"), are heart-shaped like the oars of their ancient ancestors from Israel. Their language is derived from Hebrew. In Kashmir, under the name of Yuz Asaf, it is said that Jesus sought out one of Judea's Lost Tribes.

Crew members of "Jesus in India" wear bandanas on their heads (and one even wears a towel) to show respect and to receive permission to film at the Golden Temple.

"Jesus in India" Filming Team Members were guests at the statehouse in Goa, India, and from there they journeyed to visit the Basilica of St. Francis Xavier, whose body is uncorrupted after hundreds of years.

Paul Davids rests on the ground while on a search in Calcutta for Disciples of Swami Abhedananda, who translated the ancient scrolls at Hemis Monastery that describe young Jesus' travels in India.

10. I Learn About the *Talmud of Jmmanuel*

> *Nothing stands in the way of an Earthhuman's*
> *spiritual progress, but the Earthhuman himself*
> —Semjase, purported visitor from
> Pleiades star system

From the age of thirteen onwards, whenever I visited a bookstore, I always asked the clerk "Where are the UFO books?" Through the years, I bought and read dozens of UFO books, practically every one I could find. But despite the wonderfully tolerant and broad-minded attitude of my parents, I got a lot of criticism and ridicule from many other people. Young and old. Especially growing up in a small, Christian Fundamentalist community in Texas, in the Bible Belt. So I learned to clam up, conceal my thoughts and "shut down" my feelings.

Several years after I returned from that first trip to India, I was working with a small publishing company in a town in rural Illinois. It happened that the publisher had a regular subscription to the UFO Newsclipping Service from Lucius Farish. Published out of Arkansas, I eagerly looked forward to reading it each month.

After work one day, I was reading the UFO Newsclipping Service and came across a book review of **Light Years** by Gary Kinder, published by Atlantic Monthly Press of New York. The book review was by a newspaper reporter who seemed to have an arrogant attitude. It was as if he were cynically thinking "I don't think this could possibly be true, so I'll ridicule this book."

Light Years tells the story of Eduard Albert "Billy" Meier, a one-armed, German-speaking Swiss farmer of very limited formal education, who claims he has been meeting with human beings from the Pleiades, a cluster of the "Seven Sister Stars" almost five hundred light years away. Billy, who lost one arm in an accident long ago, provided the most remarkable still photos (that he had taken) of UFO's or "flying saucers" ever seen, literally hundreds of color photos in the Swiss Alps, including 8mm motion picture film, taken long before the digital film revolution that brought us Adobe Photoshop and all sorts of computer manipulation of images.

Billy insists that he was told that the humans from the Pleiades make the journey in about seven hours. About three and a half hours are needed to reach the threshold of light speed, says Billy. Then the beamship is converted to an energy configuration, attached to tachyons and sent through hyperspace to a pre-determined destination. The vast bulk of the distance is covered in a tiny fraction of a second. The beamship exits hyperspace, re-converts to physical matter, then slows down for three and a half hours to reach Earth.

At face value, it certainly sounds like pure science-fiction.

But is it?

Even "orthodox" ufologists, researchers who devote their lives to studying evidence of UFO's, dismissed Billy Meier's photos from the start because they were simply "too good." However, no one was ever able to convincingly demonstrate how a one-armed man could have faked such photos and film, and there are numerous other witnesses in Switzerland to the "scout craft" and "beam ships."

After reading the review, I got into my car and drove about a hundred miles, searching until I found a bookstore that had a copy of **Light Years**. In rural Texas, a hundred miles wasn't an excessive drive to find almost anything slightly out of the ordinary. During my free time in the next five days or so, I carefully read the book in its entirety.

The Ring of Truth?

To me, given the unusual nature of my own sightings and experiences, I couldn't dismiss the book and even felt that perhaps it had the ring of truth. Later, I found other books related to the case and read them carefully. Some of these were the large picture book **UFO Contact from the Pleiades, Volume One** and (same title) **A Supplementary Investigation Report**, both by Lt. Col. Wendelle C. Stevens (U.S. Air Force, ret.). I enjoyed reading those books very much. Wendelle Stevens served in the Air Force in Alaska, where he reported he had numerous sightings of genuine UFO's (extraterrestrial craft, he claims). The military gun camera footage he and his fellow airmen filmed of these craft was sent to Washington, and then its existence was officially denied and it was never seen again. For decades he has offered UFO photos through his UFO Archives Service, and he has published numerous case reports on instances where individuals claimed to be in contact with extraterrestrial humanoids. Such cases are called "contactees," and Billy Meier fit that category.

I found several fascinating videos about the Meier case: **"Beamship, the Meier Chronicles"** and also **"Beamship, the Movie Footage"** and **"Beamship, Metal Analysis."** I watched and re-watched the videos many times and was intrigued. I particularly liked to watch **"The Meier Chronicles"** and ponder over what Billy Meier claimed were the spiritual teachings from the Pleiadians.

I loaned that video to quite a few people, including to a chapter of MUFON (the Mutual UFO Network), which showed it at one of their meetings. I was told later that in the last five minutes of the video, when one of the beamships is hovering in the distance, perhaps two hundred yards away, and the camera zooms in on the ship, a professional photographer in the audience jumped to his feet. They said he began cursing and yelling that the footage was real, that it was a large object at a considerable distance from the camera!

I later found a documentary about the case called **"Contact."** I loaned this to a lot of friends, also. It gives an overview about the Billy Meier Case. Later, I found a series of audio cassettes which were made by Randolph Winters. The cassettes are adapted from material in the Contact Notes, which are about 1,800 pages of what is purported to be the transcripts of the conversations between the people from the Pleiades and Billy Meier. I listened to the cassettes with great interest.

Also, I repeatedly watched a video made by Randolph Winters called **"The Pleiadian Connection."** I was later able to meet Randolph Winters and hear him give some public talks. Then I was able to buy volume one of the *Contact Notes*, published by Col. Wendelle Stevens. I was enthusiastic to read the material.

Later, I bought and read volumes two, three, and four of the *Contact Notes*. The material is challenging, to say the least. But is it true? Or is it what researchers would call a "red herring," something that distracts us from and pulls us away from the "real" body of evidence we ought to be studying?

If you tend to accept it, the impression must be that it is marvelous, as well as deeply spiritual and inspiring. It also has the appearance of being both scientific and insightful.

If you tend to reject it, nevertheless it teases the intellect and confronts our assumptions about reality, as well as challenging one's thinking at every level. Even a staunch skeptic, I should think, would find the degree of detail and appearance of sincerity and credibility an enormous tease to the intellect.

Several times I was able to attend talks given by Guido Moosbrugger, a close friend and confidant of Billy Meier, who lived at the Meier farm. Moosbrugger claims that he has also been an eyewitness of the Pleiadian beam-ships, and one of his photographs of a beam-ship appears in the book **Light Years**. He has also written a German language book about the case called **And Still They Fly**, which has been translated into English.

Later, I met Billy Meier's son, Methusalem, who gave an intriguing speech at the International UFO Congress at Laughlin, Nevada. During the week-long conference we spoke frequently about his father's experiences. Phobol Cheng of Cambodia, who is a representative to the United Nations, also spoke at the conference. She presented first-person testimony of the UFO sightings and contacts she witnessed as a teenager while living at the Ashoka Ashram in India. Those events were in connection with Billy Meier who was studying there at that time with her grandfather.

So what could I conclude? Here was a case of a man who had UFO sightings in his youth, but his experiences with that realm of the "paranormal" did not end there. It's where they began.

In my own case I had had an inexplicable sighting in my youth, and after my hypnotic regression experience with Dr. Leo Sprinkle, I had the distinct impression that my close brush with this phenomenon did not end there, either.

So could visits by humanoid beings from the Pleiades be real? And was there any interaction between this sort of phenomena and some of the Biblical accounts of so-called miracles?

The more that I read and found out about the case, the more "gross consistencies" (to use investigator Tom Welch's phrase) I found in the Billy Meier material.

Time Travel?

At one point, I read an issue of a magazine published by Randolph Winters called **"Contact, Erra to Terra."** Some advertising told about a series of cassette tapes which included one with the following write-up:

"Jmmanuel (Jesus Christ) and the Concept of God. Jmmanuel the man, known as Jesus Christ. Who was he and what did he really teach? Billy Meier was allowed to travel back in time to the year 32 and talk with Jmmanuel about his mission and how it relates to our future. From the book called **The Talmud**

Jmmanuel *(the original writings of Jmmanuel), a discussion of the story of Easter. Was Jesus really the son of god? The Pleiadian concept of gods, and their cognitions of Creation."*

I tend to be rather broad-minded and flexible in my thinking, as the reader is well aware by now. But at first glance, here Billy Meier was crossing a line that I did not think could be crossed. It strained his credibility, to say the least. Worse than "strained" – it seemed to stretch whatever credibility he might have had to the bursting point. I was kind of boggled by the concept that time travel really could be possible, but for some reason it rather irritated me to think that Billy Meier could have the audacity to assert that he had gone back in time and met Jesus Christ himself and had a conversation with him. How could any rational person accept this, even for a moment? Let's not even address the problems of simultaneous translation of ancient Aramaic or Hebrew into contemporary Swiss German. (Well, the Pleiadians can perhaps accomplish anything, Billy would say. Most of us have just not been fortunate enough to meet them.)

Still, in those few moments when I actually let myself contemplate this, my reaction was envy over the notion of someone from our time actually getting to meet Jesus in his time! A tantalizing thought or fantasy, but one that I felt the need to dismiss as impossible, as most every "sane" person would.

It's fine to be open-minded, but not so open-minded that one's brain turns to mush. And why was Billy Meier, whose accounts of his other-worldly experiences seemed to be such a substantive puzzle, undermining his credibility by making such a claim?

In September, 1992, I happened to be listening one evening to National Public Radio. The program was **"As It Happens"** with Alan Maipland and Geoffrey Stevens. They were interviewing Dr. David Doitch, one of the world's leading physicists at Oxford University in England. They were talking about *a future quantum mechanical view*. Specifically, they were talking about time travel!

Dr. Doitch said: "Once a thing has been shown to be possible in physics, technology soon follows."

He explained that regarding time travel, scientists in 1992, were possibly at a comparable point to scientists in the 1930s when they were only three or four years away from the invention of television! They first knew that television was possible, and then they built the technology. He explained that once the theoretical constructs are worked out, and scientists know something is "do-able," then within a few years or decades, the actual device will be built. Mankind's visit to the moon at the end of the 1960's was a prime example. The interviewer asked: "Will time travel become a reality?"

David Doitch's answer: "Yes, certainly!"

That interview certainly got my attention. It woke me up to unconsidered possibilities. As I thought more about it, the concept did not seem so crazy. Why couldn't it be possible? Why did reality have to conform to my own limited expectations? Lots of people I deal with do not believe in space aliens, out of body experiences, remote viewing, reincarnation, karma, telepathy or anything of a so-called paranormal nature. Consequently, they remain closed in their thinking and don't read or watch anything that would challenge their narrow view. However, their closed-mindedness doesn't make such beliefs wrong.

History provides many examples. One of the most salient is the conflict a few hundred years ago between Galileo and the Catholic Church. Galileo was subjected to house arrest for holding opinions that we know today are scientifically correct. A few centuries later, the Pope of the "infallible" church issued an apology to the long-deceased Galileo and reversed course.

Certainly the debunkers have had their field day with Billy Meier, and just because controversy surrounds his mind-boggling claims does not make him another Galileo, meaning correct yet persecuted. Controversy surrounds frauds, too. However, I had to take the position, after hearing Dr. David Doitch, that the verdict is not yet in on any of these matters.

Though skepticism is a reasonable position to take much of the time, closed-mindedness cuts off the possibility of discovery and human growth. Regarding closed-mindedness, the Hindus call it "the warehousing of a soul," a situation in which the soul is not attempting to grow spiritually. There is no attempt to gain knowledge and wisdom, to seek and discern truth.

As the Hindus view life, the whole purpose of being incarnate in a human body is to evolve spiritually, to seek wisdom and truth, and to incorporate wisdom and truth into one's daily life. Or as the Pleiadians might put it (if one allows oneself the luxury of suspending disbelief regarding Billy Meier), the important thing is to learn about Creation and its laws, and to live and evolve in harmony with Creation. To evolve spiritually, we have to make mistakes and learn from them.

Billy Meier, in the spirit of an intellectual revolution, claims that the Pleiadians say that a "power elite" has basically had a stranglehold on the masses of Earth people for thousands of years. The "power elite" does not want people to grow spiritually, because then they might develop intuitive, telepathic, and other abilities which would empower them. People then would be fearless and could not be controlled by the government (be it a public government or secret government) or anyone else. People might also then discern truth from falsehood and recognize the false "belief systems" which have been foisted upon them to control them. So says Billy Meier. And according to Meier, so say his friends from the Pleiades star system.

The Talmud of Jmmanuel

I listened attentively to the cassettes about Jmmanuel. Knowing my curiosity and interests, what choice did I have but seek out ***The Talmud of Jmmanuel***, published by Steelmark Publishing, of Mounds, Oklahoma (www.steelmarkonline.com).

So I offer my reader, for better or worse, some basic information about ***The Talmud of Jmmanuel*** (known as the TJ) so that one might come to some sort of informed opinion about the matter and the controversy.

The TJ is purported to be an ancient Aramaic document discovered in 1963 by Billy Meier in the form of scrolls encased in preservative resin. According to Meier's account, this was after a Greek Orthodox priest named Isa Rashid discovered the actual burial cave of Jmmanuel (Jesus Christ). The scrolls, which Meier claims were buried under a flat rock in the tomb, were later purportedly translated from Aramaic into German by Isa Rashid and edited and encoded by Eduard Albert "Billy" Meier, whose native language is German.

Yes, admittedly, it sounds too good to be true. However, this is only where the tale begins. There is much more.

Biblical scholars have long been searching for what they call the "Q" document, and most seem convinced that "Q" does exist or at least at one time, about two thousand years ago, did exist. "Q" is purported to be the earliest version of New Testament scripture and of the Jesus story, a document to which the writers of Matthew, Mark, Luke and John of the New Testament could have all had access. In this way, similarities between the Gospels are explained (they all are adaptations of the same source) and so are the differences.

But no one has ever found "Q." Among all the ancient Gospels (the so-called apocryphal texts) that have been unearthed, "Q" has not been among them. So "Q" remains a tempting theory, unproven but believed to exist by many top Biblical scholars.

Could Billy Meier's TJ have been the missing "Q" document? Or is someone having a cruel joke on us, trying to toy with those among us gullible enough to tend to believe it? We do not know.

However, I say about this the same as I've always said about all things worthy of investigation and consideration: dismiss it out of hand only at your own risk. (And if it is to be dismissed, let's do so with some education about what it purports to be and what it says.)

I frequently read the Gospels during my childhood and early adult years and had always felt as if they had been tampered with or altered somehow. The TJ, for me, was worthy of study and investigateon. Did it have the ring of truth? Or was this a wild goose chase, a temptation to someone such as myself who had long been on a personal search to solve certain mysteries of the Bible. I took the bait, at least to consider it. It was while I was reading the latter part of the TJ, that I came across material which told specific details about events following the crucifixion.

Some of those details – more than a few of them – lined up rather well with some of the conclusions I'd come to as a result of my studies of Jesus in India. In other words, there was a confluence with much of the strange quest I had been on since stumbling upon Murree Beer in the bar in the American Embassy Annex in Afghanistan.

To summarize a few of the links: The TJ states that Jmmanuel (Jesus) had been in a state of near-death on the cross but did not actually die. And post-crucifixion, after Jmmanuel had been laid out in Joseph of Arimathea's tomb (as recounted in the New Testament), the TJ adds that when Joseph of Arimathea returned with friends of Jmmanuel's from India, they entered the tomb through a secret, back tunnel entrance. The men from India were healers; they brought special salves and medicines and ministered to Jmmanuel for three days. After that time, the TJ states that he was strong enough to walk.

Of relevance to this: the noted, ancient historian Josephus recounts a true story about an occasion when he was returning to Jerusalem and found that three of his friends had been crucified by the Romans. Josephus went immediately to his friend the governor Tiberius, who granted his request and had the three men taken down from the crosses. And one of the three men survived! The point is that despite the excruciating ordeal, some people have survived a crucifix-

I Learn About the Talmud of Jmmanuel 169

ion. For additional details, see *Celestial Teachings* by Dr. James Deardorff.

In fact, it has been reported in various news stories that survival of crucifixion has been repeatedly demonstrated in the Philippines, where on occasion devotees have voluntarily been subjected to crucifixion on Easter, with nails driven through the hands and feet.

The details about Jmmanuel in *The Talmud of Jmmanuel* further state that he recuperated in hiding in Damascus for about two years. During that time, he was joined there by his mother, Mary, his brother Thomas, his disciple and close friend, Judas Iscariot, and others.

Of significant importance: the TJ makes it clear that Judas Iscariot, the treasurer, one of the twelve Apostles, was not the betrayer of Jmmanuel. The purported translation of the text of the TJ makes clear that the real betrayer was named Juda Ihariot, the son of Pharisee Simeon. After Juda Ihariot's suicide, Jesus' enemies had the names switched and spread the false rumor. The lie implied: "One of his own people betrayed him, so how can his teachings have any worth?"

Also, according to the account in this purportedly ancient document (which was purportedly destroyed in a raid on the Palestine refugee camp where it was being diligently translated by Isa Rashid), it was Jmmanuel himself, in his flesh-and-blood body, who confronted Saul of Tarsus (later to become Saint Paul) one night on the road leading to Damascus. In the New Testament, Paul describes a rather ethereal Jesus that he encountered, as bright as the sun, so one would have to allow for considerable exaggeration on the part of Paul (or on the part of the Biblical writers who wrote the lines attributed to Paul) to accept that it was in fact a flesh-and-blood Jesus (rather than a spiritual vision) that Saul of Tarsus saw.

There is a significant conflict here with the canonical Gospels. However, for further details, read the complete account in *The Talmud of Jmmanuel*, Chapter 33, page 267. Briefly, what the TJ claims (or rather, what Billy Meier claims in offering up his German version of the TJ which no longer exists) is that Jmmanuel prepared a concoction of chemicals (a.k.a. fireworks) and ignited them at night, temporarily blinding Saul. Jmmanuel also spoke sternly to Saul before slipping away.

Of incidental note, the TJ contains an earlier passage in which Jmmanuel and Saul had a face-to-face meeting one night with a heated exchange of words. At the end, Jmmanuel picked up a stick and chased

Saul away! And then Saul, his thoughts on revenge, met with Juda Ihariot (the real betrayer, according to the TJ), the son of the Pharisee Simeon, to discuss how to seize Jmmanuel and turn him over to the authorities. See Chapter 26, page 201, in the TJ for the entire passage. According to the New Testament, of course, Saul of Tarsus (in which he becomes "St. Paul"), until his conversion was a rather cold-blooded persecutor of Christians and even a brutal murderer of defenseless Christian men, women and children. Ironically, as we all know, Christianity completely accepts and embraces the persecutor Saul's transformation into Saint Paul, long ago having elevated him to both hero and role model and authority on the precepts of Christ, because he converted and accepted the divinity of Jesus.

Thus, the TJ gives a rather more "earth-bound" interpretation of how it was that Saul met up with Jmmanuel (Jesus) on the road to Damascus after the crucifixion.

Returning to India

To continue with Biblical events as purportedly described in the TJ, following his two years in Damascus, Jmmanuel and his close group joined a caravan journeying to India. The TJ states that it was in what is now northern Pakistan that Jmmanuel's mother, Mary (then advanced in years) became very ill and died.

As the reader well knows by now, the town of Murree, Pakistan, in the Himalayan foothills, is named for Mary's burial place. What is locally claimed to be her tomb can still be visited today, or at least it could be visited until relatively recently. Today it is behind barbed wire at a military base and is located precisely within the footings of a tall television tower. Ironically, this serves to protect it.

As skeptical as I might like to be of the TJ and the story of how Billy Meier came across the document in the Holy Land, the interconnections of the TJ's story of Mary's death on Jesus' trip back to India and my own research on that matter was too much to expect me to ignore. Unless, of course, the TJ has been concocted in modern times by someone who followed the same trail of inquiry I did across Asia, someone who came to more or less the same conclusions, deciding then to fabricate an "ancient" Biblical document to back up the story. It is regrettable that it will never be possible to examine the purported document, which, it is claimed, was destroyed during an Israeli air raid on a Palestinian refugee camp.

Are there shades of anti-semitism in this story? And does that make it all the more likely that it's an elaborate concoction? Or is there no good reason why the story of how the TJ was found and translated could not simply be true?

Fact or fraud, one or the other must ultimately be the case. We do not have an answer. We do not even have a photograph of the TJ document to lend support to the story that it really did exist. However, before we try to make up our minds on the matter of fact or fraud, we should hold our fire a bit longer, because there's still more.

The remainder of the TJ story is that following his mother's death, Jmmanuel went to Srinagar, Kashmir, in northwestern India. There, at about the age of 45, he married a pretty, young woman and they settled down to a happy married life. The woman bore him several children, the oldest of which was a boy named Joseph. Jmmanuel continued to go on journeys, give spiritual teachings and perform healings throughout his lifetime.

So the TJ not only conforms with the findings I stumbled upon (from the day I drank that Murree Beer forward to the present), but it also places a post-crucifixion Jesus in Srinagar, the very location of the tomb of Yuz Asaf. In movies and mystery stories, they always say at a point like this, "The plot thickens." I hate to repeat a cliché, so let me merely say this left me in the thickets – the thickets of an ever-deepening mystery that not only involved a Biblical mystery but also a one-armed farmer from Switzerland (Billy Meier) who purports to be on close terms with human-like aliens from the Pleiades star system.

Had I taken a very wrong turn? How did I end up here?

However, as for the TJ, I had to read on, and read on I certainly did. In the TJ, Judas Iscariot is presented as Jmmanuel's neighbor and close friend. He frequently accompanied Jmmanuel on his journeys and was his diligent scribe. He died at about the age of ninety and was also buried near Srinagar. Jmmanuel lived to about the age of one hundred ten and was buried at Srinagar.

This of course conflicts with yet another account on Judas, one that we know is very ancient. I am referring, of course, to the ***Gospel of Judas***, for which translation was completed relatively recently. That apocryphal gospel portrays Judas as the "betrayer" but only at Jesus' request. Rather than being the embodiment of evil (that provoked centuries of anti-Semitism), Judas in the ***Gospel of Judas*** turns Jesus over to the Romans, because that's what Jesus demanded and required. The Jesus presented in that account is a prophet who knew full well he could not complete his mission, unless his final confrontation with his accusers played out to its conclusion. His mission required self-sacrifice and giving up the body ("the clothes that cover my spirit," says Jesus in the **Gospel of Judas**).

So we now have three choices of how to regard the Judas story. The version in the TJ (Judas never did the deed history accuses him of doing, and he was framed), the version in the Gospel of Judas (Judas did it but only on Jesus' orders) and the New Testament version (Judas was the betrayer of Jesus).

Do we have any basis to make a choice between the three? Do we automatically revert to the easiest course, to simply believe what is in the canonical Gospels, even though Matthew, Mark, Luke and John were written long after the crucifixion… perhaps forty years or more afterwards?

Permit me to continue with the TJ account of the life of Jmmanuel by focusing on acts attributed in the TJ to Jmmanuel's eldest son, Joseph. Following his father Jmmanuel's (Jesus') death, his son Joseph took the scrolls of parchment, which contained the **Talmud of Jmmanuel** encased in resin, and he traveled to Jerusalem. There, in the burial cave in which Jmmanuel had lain, Joseph buried the scrolls under a rock within the cave which was partially filled in with sand and dirt. He believed that would be the safest and most appropriate place for history eventually to find the document and try to come to terms with its account.

According to Eduard Albert "Billy" Meier's claims, in 1963 he was directed to find the scrolls (with a little help from his extraterrestrial "friends" from the Pleiades Star System), and with the assistance of Priest Isa Rashid the scrolls were translated from Aramaic to German. Isa Rashid, says Meier, and his family were later killed by Israeli security forces and history was denied examination of the TJ, which was incinerated.

I will be the first to acknowledge that I do not have the scholarly qualifications to determine whether this TJ episode is the greatest Biblical discovery of modern times or whether it is a crock and fiasco that distracts from all the more credible findings on the issues this book addresses.

So do not look to me for the answer you seek on this particular question. But there is a professor to whom I can refer you if you wish to dig deeper. That man is Dr. James Deardorff, author of **Celestial Teachings**, a rather "revolutionary" and extraordinary attempt to prove, using Biblical scholarship, that the ***Talmud of Jmmanuel*** story is true. ***Celestial Teachings*** is a verse-by-verse comparison and analysis of the ***Gospel of Matthew*** and ***The Talmud of Jmmanuel.***

Also of importance and value is the version of ***The Talmud of Jmmanuel*** translated into English by Julie H. Ziegler and B.L. Greene.

Dr. James Deardorff, who began as a skeptic, reached the opposite conclusion by the end of his year of analysis of the translation of the TJ. He purports that ***The Talmud of Jmmanuel*** really is the original, uncensored ***Gospel of Matthew.*** (He also concludes, contrary to most scholars, that the ***Gospel of Matthew*** preceded the Gospel of Mark rather than the other way around.)

Dr. Deardorff is mindful that ***The Talmud of Jmmanuel*** would be rejected immediately by most Christians, who would consider it totally heretical. However Dr. Deardoff's conclusion is that the Gospel of Matthew is a censored, redacted and sanitized version of the TJ, and that the TJ is not some fraud or concoction. Dr. Deardorff's book, ***Celestial Teachings***, mentioned above, gives the proposed scholarly explanations for this theory.

Let's be frank about the extent to which Billy Meier has been eviscerated by the naysayers. He has been scathingly attacked by skeptics, and I leave it to my readers to conclude on their own whether those attacks are justified. Nevertheless, I must mention Kal K. Korff, a debunker who makes masses of claims against the reality of Billy Meier's contact experiences, and by extrapolation, he is just as harsh in his opinion of the TJ. Please take note that Dr. James W. Deardorff has written a well-researched and scholarly report in 1996 entitled ***A Refutation of False Claims and Distortions by Korff.***

As for me, what do I make of this additional controversy, one that I certainly did not need? I profess a certain exasperation. The will to believe unwarranted things is an ever-present danger and one to which we are all susceptible. Yet it is an undeniable historical fact that time and again the mass of mankind has been confronted with many examples of truth and has utterly missed the point and chosen falsehood. Jesus cited himself as an example. The builders rejected the cornerstone, he said. And as history has proven, he turned out to be a rather persuasive cornerstone, in spite of his fate on the cross.

Galileo had his problems with the "enlightened" Pope of his day, who considered himself infallible and received all knowledge directly from God, including the knowledge that Galileo was a heretic and on his way to hellfire for his utterly wrong-headed views of the puny place of the Earth in the solar system.

Also, let's consider the Wright Brothers. The story that their contraption had flown was widely disbelieved by a skeptical public. The U.S. military, in its infinite wisdom, pronounced that the airplane had "no sound military application" and therefore rejected it. No research and development money for that!

And so, like always, I find myself once again at a difficult – painstakingly difficult – intellectual crossroads. Maybe there is some merit to the **Talmud of Jmmanuel** and all of Billy Meier's claims. Maybe it is all real and settles many dimensions of the Jesus mystery and the mystery of man's place in the cosmos, in relation to other advanced civilizations spread out across the galaxy. But just remember, I didn't claim to you it's true. I just informed you that it has been claimed. And I suggested you make a date with Dr. James Deardorff (www.tjresearch.info). Look up his writings and give him a few hours of your time. And then you take it from there. Make up your own mind, if you can.

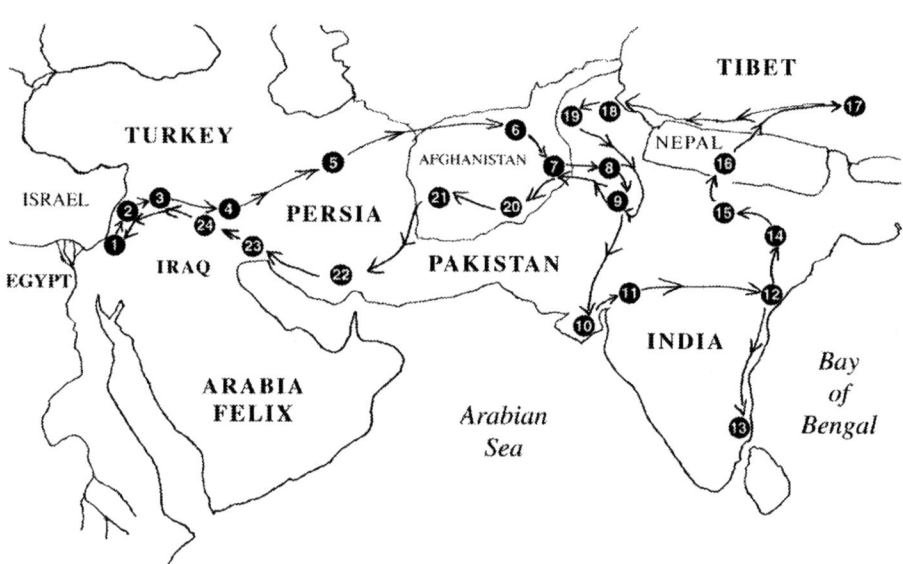

Jesus' Travels on the Silk Road and Beyond?

11. How Do You Like Your Jesus?

> *When you tell the truth to someone, you should first have one foot in the stirrup of your horse.*
> —Turkish saying

How do you like your coffee? With cream or milk? With sugar? Black? How do you like your ice cream? With chocolate syrup? With nuts? With fruit?

How do you like your Jesus?

I grew up in a Fundamentalist Christian church in which it seemed to me that most of the preachers and elders talked far more about the Apostle Paul than about Jesus. Personally, I loved to really focus on Jesus: his life, his teachings and his miracles.

However, somehow I always felt intuitively that I wasn't getting the whole, true story. It seemed to me as if I was being offered a certain amount of deception and censorship. The problem of the eighteen missing years compounded all the other problems of credibility for me.

Think about it: do we grasp the potential significance of those missing years in the life of Jesus? The teenage years and twenties years are critically important for growth and the development of one's values and personality.

The only transitional verse in the Bible dealing with the missing years comes at the end of the second chapter of Luke (Luke 2:52). These are the fourteen words, **"And Jesus increased in wisdom and stature, and in favor with God and man."**

What is that supposed to mean?

Does it mean that for many years Jesus was just humming away in his father's carpentry shop, making chairs and tables? And Jesus magically was gaining great spiritual wisdom by going for long walks in the hills? And the next chapter in Luke begins with Jesus being baptized by John and then beginning his ministry at age thirty.

Almost everyone conveniently overlooks a very important point about ancient Jewish culture: Jewish boys at the age of thirteen years (when they officially "become a man" in a Bar Mitzvah ceremony) in those days were expected to take a wife reasonably soon thereafter! In particular, boys who would become rabbis or teachers were expected to marry! Therefore, there would be tremendous social pressure for a brilliant and very promising boy such as Jesus to marry. A family's reputation was at stake. Such a boy who did not marry could be considered immoral and very strange, or worse!

The simple solution for a very special boy such as Jesus, who had different plans and goals, was to depart from home, either secretly or with his family's blessing. Jesus had other siblings, with normal goals, who would stay at home. Jesus could have written a goodbye letter, telling that he would return after some years. Then he could have joined a camel caravan of merchants, bound for India. With Jesus physically absent, his parents could make up any respectable story they wanted to tell people—and the pressure would be off.

To me, the missing time following the feast of the Passover, when Jesus was twelve, followed by the jump to the year when he began his ministry, seems not to be an accidental omission, nor a mere lack of information due to no such information about the life of Jesus being available to the Biblical writers.

I know that some scholars (such as Prof. Alan C. Mitchell of the Georgetown University Department of Divinity) insist that no such information was ever available to the writers of the Bible. Some scholars conclude that the Biblical birth narrative about Jesus is essentially fiction, and that therefore there is <u>no</u> wealth of <u>real</u> historical information about the earliest years of Jesus that would contrast with the absence of information on the years up to age thirty.

However, to me all of this scholarly dispute has little result other than to serve as a sort of erudite smokescreen for the missing information in the Bible. To me, this has always had the appearance of a blatantly obvious coverup.

Thus, for most of my life, I have asked for a resolution to the issue of what precisely is being covered up. Usually cover-ups result when someone with knowledge or information wants to withhold it. It's fine for them to know, but not okay for you to be told or find out.

My conclusion has always been that someone deliberately never put the "lost years" into any of the Gospels. Why?

Here we enter the realm of conjecture.

So I will conjecture.

If the Christian Bible were to have explicitly stated that Jesus Christ went to India, that he lived there for years and actively studied Hinduism, Buddhism and Jainism, that would show unequivocally that Jesus was interested in other religions. Perhaps he was even respectful of other religions! And if the Bible were to reveal that Jesus learned healing arts from Hindu holy people, that might be seen as detracting from some of Christianity's central themes. In India, the Hindus believe in miracles too. They believe that certain of their saints have walked on water, appeared in multiple places at the same time, survived certain death by stopping their hearts and even submitted to burial, only to "return to life." We Christians have a New Testament in which the Lord walks on water, makes five loaves feed five thousand people, helps the blind to see and performs many other miraculous events. If the miracle of enabling the blind to see were explained as a form of ancient Hindu cataract surgery using obsidian blades, the status of Christianity might be profoundly tainted or changed. Christianity asserts that some mud or spittle from Jesus, applied to the eye of the blind, triggered the miracle that enabled the blind to see.

"Do not go where the Bible does not go." That's what I was taught as a Fundamentalist Christian growing up. "Do not add one word to the Bible and do not subtract a word. It is the infallible word of God."

Some denominations of Christianity, beginning with the Unitarians, long ago dispensed with this literalist way of thinking. But this kind of thinking prevails, largely unquestioned, throughout much of the Fundamentalist Bible Belt in the United States, where I was raised. What happens the moment the questioning and analysis begins? Well, some would say mockingly that you begin by questioning your faith, and you end up, if you give any credence to the one-armed farmer from Switzerland, on a spaceship from the Pleiades traveling back in time to ancient Jerusalem or struggling to interpret a purportedly ancient document called ***The Talmud of Jmmanuel*** that no longer even exists because it's claimed it was bombed in a Palestinian refugee camp (and which may never have really existed at all). Questions such as the ones I asked, that set me out upon my journey, make you persona non grata. They get you "dis-fellowshipped" from your church.

But asking these questions and examining them does not automatically mean that we need to accept the most extreme conclusions, for example by embracing the claims of Billy Meier (though that is our option if we choose to do so and if our life experiences lead us to give credence to his claims.) The questions are discouraged, however, and the missing years of Jesus are avoided from all discourse, because accepting less miraculous explanations for the miracles of Jesus, from the healing of the blind to appearing before the Apostles after his crucifixion, ultimately could change many things in the religion.

Let's begin by stating that the status of Christian priests and preachers could be changed! Shall we continue the analysis of the repercussions or just avoid the journey so you can fill in the blanks?

I'll fill in a few of them.

It's no secret that churches are keenly interested in getting people's contributions. If you have any doubts about that, go visit a city with some Christian universities and spend some time in the Christian nursing homes and hospitals. You will see what some cynical people might refer to as "religious vultures" wooing elderly people to will their homes, businesses, ranches (or all of the above) to specific church groups and organizations.

I am personally familiar with cases where those efforts by religious organizations have proven highly effective, sometimes persuading infirm or ill elderly people who may not be in possession of all of their faculties. This is sometimes done for the benefit of religious institutions in spite of the fact that it is to the severe detriment of surviving family members.

To the extent that churches are structured – in fact organized religion itself is structured – to increase the power of the churches and religions over their adherents, the message always has to be very carefully filtered and controlled.

Is this religion? Spirituality? Or is it an exercise in social and political power and unadulterated materialism?

Whatever we call it, it's a facet of human behavior that helps explain why the Gospels apparently were not faithful to their original source.

As author Janet Bock points out in her book **The Jesus Mystery**: "In examining historical records of the early Christian church, it became evident that early church councils, especially the First Council of Nicea in 325 A.D., changed many points of doctrine, and it was possible those missing years were expunged because they did not coincide with the political needs of a growing church."

The Power Elite and Belief Systems

Consider the following point of view. It doesn't originate with me, and I'm not the first who has proposed it. In fact, I am not proposing it, merely asking you to consider it. It's like John Lennon's unforgettable song **"Imagine."** He says "Imagine there's no heaven. It's easy if you try. No hell below us. Above us only sky."

That's the world according to John Lennon. He doesn't say he believes it. He only asks you to imagine it.

Try imagining this: For thousands of years on planet Earth a "power elite" has controlled earth humans by foisting "belief systems" (and that would include systems of government as well as organized religions) upon the masses of people. Those belief systems are often to the detriment of the people: they keep people disempowered and in spiritual darkness.

The power elite are delighted with that situation. That is what they want. People who are disempowered can easily be controlled, exploited and manipulated! The power elite are content to keep a low profile and basically stay out of public view—and public scrutiny!

The effect of the belief systems is something like: "Okay, you peasants and serfs! Obey your king or you will rot in the dungeon! Obey Holy Mother Church or you will burn in Hell for Eternity!" Of course, the common people are frightened by this! They hustle to conform, to be submissive and certainly to avoid rocking the boat!

The thing the power elite does not want, the thing they dread and consider most odious, is for people to become spiritually empowered. When people are genuinely seeking truth and evolving spiritually, they will develop strong intuitive abilities. With those abilities, they will much more easily discern truth from falsehood. They will know when their leaders and governments are lying to them.

Continue imagining and imagine this. Governments on this planet are primarily in the hands of power-hungry, arrogant people who seek to dominate, control, exploit and manipulate masses of people and natural resources. Now imagine the converse: that governments exist that try to help people grow spiritually and assist them in that direction – that governments want people to live according to the laws of Creation, and instead of laws they give people what could be called suggestions or examples.

If I haven't lost you up until this point, surely you're thinking I've lost you now. Surely I must be dreaming. These imaginings I've offered up have gone from the likely to the impossible.

But here is a truth I've gleaned from my quest and my travels, and call it a mere dream if you like, but then it is a truthful dream:

As people evolve spiritually they will become more and more fearless. They will be less subject to intimidation and threats. Spiritual empowerment may also include enhanced telepathic abilities, clairvoyance, telekinesis and other abilities. All in all, a human population which is really starting to evolve spiritually will not only be more empowered, they will be more ethical, much less prone to violence and warfare and keenly concerned about the environment. They will also become insightful thinkers!

So how do you like your Jesus? Let's talk a little about Divinity, Salvation and Resurrection. Big subjects. Hot potatoes! Yes, they are touchy, very important and sensitive issues because they are parts of the most cherished beliefs of most Christians. And roughly speaking, when we count Protestants and Catholics, we may be talking about approximately 1,000,000,000 (one billion) to 1,400,000,000 people on planet Earth who consider themselves Christians, of some sort.

Jesus Was An Extraordinary Human Being

Continue imagining. Imagine that Jesus was a human being – quite a bit more extraordinary than you and I, but a human being nevertheless – biologically "ordinary." He was very spiritually advanced and possessed great knowledge and wisdom. Perhaps this even enabled him to perform what we call "miracles" – or perhaps there are other explanations for the stories of miracles that are imbedded throughout the Bible, both Old Testament and New.

Imagine that Jesus did not wish to be worshipped or treated as the only begotten Son of God. (The Bible says Jesus said "The things that I do you shall do also, and even greater things.") Imagine that Jesus was not peddling salvation, scaring people with hellfire or demanding money (except for direct benefit to the poor, sick and downtrodden).

He did want people to listen to his teachings about Creation and its laws. He wanted people to think for themselves, to use logic and reason, and to seek knowledge and wisdom.

He wanted people to learn from their mistakes and to grow spiritually. He wanted people to get in touch with their eternal souls which are omnipotent. He wanted to be an example for people.

He also wanted people to have a correct relationship with God ("Our Father who art in heaven, hallowed be Thy name.")

However, by this process of imagining, he was a man – a man who could have survived a crucifixion that was not continued to its ultimate outcome. (His legs were not broken, which hastens death. He was on the cross a short time – many prisoners have survived the cross much longer. Besides, in modern medicine, haven't we established that it's not always clear when a patient has "flat-lined"? Aren't there many credible examples of people given up for dead who proved themselves alive before being put into coffins?)

By this process of imagining – of reasoning really – the point is he could have been a man who spent much of his youth in a foreign country... probably India... and who returned to his homeland as a thirty year old man to preach and teach and heal.

By this reasoning (with apologies to those who debunk the so-called "swoon" theories), he could have still been alive when meeting with his Apostles, post-crucifixion, and he could have embarked on travel back to India to escape the cruel and ruthless Roman Empire, taking his mother Mary with him. He did send Thomas to India. This we know. Pope John Paul II acknowledged this in going to India to pay respects to Apostle Thomas at Chennai where Doubting Thomas spent twenty years preaching and where Thomas' tomb exists today.

Why India? What was its unique importance?

It was the very embodiment of two of the prevailing ancient religions: Hinduism and Buddhism. It was a spiritual center with remarkable temples and religious art and iconography. The people of India have always been largely devoted to trying to understand the meaning of life, in all its cycles. And they conceived systems of philosophy very different from those of the Greeks and Romans, who so strongly influenced the development and emerging shape of early Christianity after Christ's lifetime.

In the days following the crucifixion, for the Apostles who then remained in Judea (before dispersing to many other countries), when asked by Roman soldiers who heard rumors that Jesus (who was supposed to have been executed) was sighted with them, how would they reply? Would they have said: "Yes, you're quite correct, he's been here with us, we ate fish together and walked to Galilee." Or would they have replied: "Oh no, sir, that is impossible, sir. He is no longer on this earth. He died on the cross and his spirit has gone to the heavens. Perhaps you will find him in the clouds above, sitting at the right hand of his God, but you certainly will not find him here."

How do Christians come to terms with the tomb of Yuz Asaf? Except for the few educated about the mystery, they do not. It is ignored. People have not been told of it, or that there is evidence and there are artifacts taken from the Rozabal tomb by its Muslim neighbors. Christians have no opportunity to examine these mysteries, and for the most part they do not seem to care. Those who know about it often debunk it without inquiry. However, putting aside the theories of film producer James Cameron, who sponsored a documentary film (on the Discovery Channel) and a book asserting that Jesus' family tomb has been found in Jerusalem, the Rozabal tomb remains a greater challenge to us, in my opinion. However, to assign supreme importance to the Rozabal Tomb in Srinagar, as the likely final resting place of the prophet who was variously known as Jesus and Jmmanuel and Saint Issa and Yuz Asaf, one has to allow that Jesus must have had a life following his intended execution on the cross. One must assume that the "tomb of Mary" sheltered by the television tower and behind barbed wire in Pakistan is possibly the tomb of the mother of Jesus, and that there was never reasonable historical evidence that mother Mary was laid to rest in Ephesus, Turkey, or in Jerusalem (where there is no body in the purported tomb and she is said by Catholicism to have ascended bodily to heaven). So most Christians stop right there. At these "heresies." I certainly stopped there, too, at the beginning.

However, the challenges to conventional Christianity are real.

The carvings (apparently <u>ancient</u> carvings?) of Prophet Yuz Asaf's feet are there to be seen by the few who have braved hostility of the local Muslims to witness this at the Rozabal tomb. The carvings show the scars of the prophet's crucifixion.

Of course, I do not know when those carvings were created. The research that invites these conclusions is by no means air-tight. But it is certainly provocative. It certainly challenges us to think in new ways.

Let's now stop imagining. Let's deal with a fact.

The New Testament declares that Jesus said that a prophet is not without honor except in his own homeland, among his own people and family. Jesus therefore knew that a true prophet *is* treated with honor when he is <u>*not*</u> among his own people and family, and when he is <u>*not*</u> in his own homeland.

How did he know this and why would he say this if he did not travel?
Would he say it because he spent part of his boyhood in Egypt? Not likely.

It appears from all the evidence, from the result of the quest and journey and investigation of this book, that he could say it because he had traveled after he had indeed become a prophet. He had traveled far and wide, to many other nations and among many other peoples, during those missing years. And he had experienced *directly* that honor of which he spoke, outside his homeland.

Putting Jmmanuel (Jesus) on a Very High Pedestal

When we make Jesus the son of God, we set him up to be worshipped as God. Of course, this means we put Jesus up on a very, very high pedestal. Which means, as far as I have concluded, that his value as an example is largely destroyed. In other words, when people exalt Jesus to God-status, his human being status becomes confusing for a lot of people. Many people say something like: "Jesus could forgive and do all he did because he is the son of God, but I'm an ordinary human, so you can't expect me to forgive or behave like Jesus."

Along with the worship of Jesus as the son of God comes the big-ticket item of Salvation. Basically, the idea is to worship Jesus, call on his name, attend your church regularly, donate money to your church, try to be good, and hopefully when you die, you'll get to go to heaven. Then you can sit on a cloud and play a harp for eternity.

Does that make any sense? Some people think they can attend church once a year at Easter, call on Jesus' holy name for salvation, live like a skunk the rest of the year, and eventually go to heaven. Does that make any sense, either?

My Christmas Card Photo, taken in Srinagar a few miles away from the Rozabal Tomb – the Tomb of Yuz Asaf who is purported to be Jesus

12. Some Closing Thoughts

*If we don't change directions, we are likely
to end up where we are going.*
—Chinese folk saying

When Mahatma Gandhi was leading the non-violent movement in India for freedom from British rule, British soldiers were frequently sent to observe his public appearances. Sometimes the soldiers were sent in disguise, as spies, to report back to their superiors. Due to the multiplicity of languages spoken in India, Gandhi often gave speeches to large crowds using the English language. However, the British officers who sent soldiers as spies told them that if Gandhi speaks in English, they should move back, out of hearing range.

"Why?" asked the soldiers. "If we are being sent to spy on the man, shouldn't we listen closely to what he is saying?"

"Well, Gandhi is talking rubbish," said the officers, "and you are likely to become confused if you listen to such nonsense!"

What was the real reason for not listening? Gandhi was telling the _Truth_! And the British officers knew that in the past, soldiers who had listened to Gandhi's eloquent words changed their thinking.

The _Truth_ Gandhi spoke was compelling, and rational men and women were often won over to his side. Some British soldiers were won over by his eloquence and reasonableness. Such soldiers were often transferred to duty in other parts of the British Empire. But that didn't change the _Truth_! India eventually won her independence in 1947 through non-violent means.

Some people claim that soldiers were also sent by the Romans two thousand years ago to spy Jesus. There is a story about an aging Roman centurion named Longinus, who was often sent to spy because of his flair for languages. The story says that Longinus spoke Aramaic and Greek, as well as Latin. He was often sent in disguise to listen to the public speeches of Jesus, and he gained sympathy for the message.

Ironically, the last duty Longinus was given before his retirement was to oversee a crucifixion—Jmmanuel's crucifixion. Tradition has it that Longinus used his spear to make a wound in Jmmanuel's side, and then he quickly pronounced him dead and left with his soldiers. However, the wound may have been a superficial spear thrust to the hip. This is the centurion described in Luke as saying, "Surely, this was a righteous man" and in Matthew and Mark as saying "Truly, this was the Son of God." Professor Ravenscroft's ***Spear of Destiny*** book contains a wealth of information about Longinus' spear and its history.

The Talmud of Jmmanuel explains that Joseph of Arimathea could tell that Jmmanuel was not dead but was in a state of near-death. Knowing that, he quickly saw Pilate and obtained permission to take the body. Pilate, too, was surprised at such a quick death but gave permission. As the TJ story goes, after the body was placed in Joseph's tomb, Joseph returned quickly with Jmmanuel's friends from India who entered through the secret, tunnel entrance. They ministered to Jmmanuel and all of them left three days later. Jmmanuel fully recuperated in hiding in Damascus, later returning to India.

Orthodox Christianity, since its inception, has insisted on discouraging this kind of possibility as heretical and unthinkable, and until the relatively recent era of freedom of speech, unutterable.

Did They Stay Dead?

As a kind of mental brainstorming, let's think for a while about some famous people, both historical and fictitious, who apparently died but later were reported to still be alive. In no particular order, some of those are John Wilkes Booth, Jesse James, Adolph Hitler, Princess Anastasia, the Lone Ranger (fictitious, but interesting to think about), and of course, as we are discussing in this book, Jesus Christ (Jmmanuel) and Judas Iscariot. Naturally, the list could be made much longer. Perhaps the reader can think of a few additions to the list.

What did all these people have in common? Clearly, they all had a good reason to be dead—and to stay that way. If they in fact were not <u>really</u> dead, it would be much better for them if people continued to <u>think</u> they were dead. Obviously, they would move to a different location, or better yet, to a different part of the world. They would take a completely different name and use some kind of disguise.

For example, John Wilkes Booth, the alleged assassin of President Lincoln, was supposedly killed during a shootout at Garrett's Farm. But two of the Union soldiers who were present and examined the body signed an affidavit saying that the body was not John Wilkes Booth. The soldiers had seen Booth perform previously in a play and had met and spoken with him afterwards at a reception. The dead man, they said, was a different man than Booth. Of course, at the time, there was tremendous pressure from the public and government to quickly put the assassination of President Lincoln to rest.

About Booth, an intriguing book, **The Reincarnation of John Wilkes Booth** by Dell Leonardi, examines a case of hypnosis and past life inquiry. The individual revealed under hypnosis that he was the reincarnation of Booth. The fascinating story from this case is that Booth did not die at Garrett's Farm but escaped on a ship bound for England, boarding the boat in San Francisco, so he would never be suspected. He changed his identity and lived the rest of his life as an actor in England, eventually dying at Calais, France. Some claim he even reached India and Ceylon. In a non-electronic age, when photography was in its infancy, escaping and covering one's identity would have been much easier.

Jesse James was, and still is, a folk hero for many people. After James' death at the hands of one of his own men, persistent rumors continued to circulate well into the twentieth century that Jesse James had survived. The rumors claimed that another man had been killed and that James had escaped to start a new life in disguise.

A program on PBS Television's Nova series dealt with an inquiry into the Jesse James mystery using DNA testing after exhuming the remains of the body and the extraction of DNA material from the teeth. That DNA was compared with DNA samples given voluntarily by three of the living biological descendants of Jesse James. The results were greater than a ninety-nine per cent positive match, almost certainly proving that the body _is_ truly that of Jesse James. Thus, this was a case where the rumor of survival was proved wrong.

Another famous man whose death is clouded in mystery is Adolph Hitler. Despite the matching of dental records, some have speculated that Hitler had several doubles, and that one of those doubles met with death in the bunker and was assumed to be Hitler. Even Dwight D. Eisenhower was quoted as saying that he never believed that Hitler died on April 30, 1945, with Eva Braun in the bunker. The psychic and author Hans Holzer claimed that he had a psychic vision of Adolph Hitler escaping Germany through Spain, disguised as a priest. Others have had the same "vision" and have speculated that Hitler died later in South America from a brain tumor or cancer.

We also know that Sadam Hussein had doubles, to decrease his risk of assassination while he was in power. Of course, in the end, the real Sadam Hussein _was_ found and captured and eventually executed.

How does this history impact upon the "case" of Jesus Christ?

In the case of Jesus, the centurion who made the death determination, may have lied knowingly. The Roman soldiers serving under centurion Longinus would gladly have accepted his determination and the order to go home to a hot dinner, wine and a dry room. Remember, terribly dark storm clouds were sweeping in and a hard rain was about to begin. So is that the way it really happened?

Remember that only one of the four canonical Gospels has Jesus proclaiming on the cross, to a convict alongside him, "Today you shall join me in paradise." The other three accounts that were written about forty or fifty years after the fact don't mention that detail.

Of course the New Testament also tells us (in Matthew) that upon the death of Jesus there was an earthquake, the veil of the temple was torn asunder and in one of the four Gospels we're treated to the details of how saints rose from the dead, coming out of their graves to walk among the living.

Is that the way it happened? All things being equal, which are you more prone to believe?

Of course, all things are not equal. A billion people alive today have been indoctrinated since they were old enough to talk with the Biblical "facts." Many of them choose the earthquake at the moment of Jesus' death, and the veil of the temple being torn – and the graves opening and all those saints experiencing instant resurrection. It's unfortunate that there were no documentary filmmakers in those days to capture those highly unusual circumstances "live" on videotape. Or television, which could have shown it on instant news.

Of interesting note: some yogis in India are able to enter into a deep meditative state in which they are able to stop their heartbeat, breathing and circulation of blood. Physicians examining those yogis have proclaimed them 'dead,' only to watch them afterwards resume their body functions and come back to life. Certainly, if the thesis of this book has merit, then Jesus (Jmmanuel) had surely studied and become adept at yoga in India and could perform many yogic feats. If he wanted to appear dead, he certainly could have accomplished it.

The Truth Will Prevail

There is a beautiful saying: "The truth will prevail." Did anyone seriously think that Nelson Mandela would win? Or did anyone believe the former Soviet Union would be vanquished and broken apart? Did anyone believe the Berlin Wall would be broken down? When Rosa Parks refused to give up her seat on the bus, did anyone believe her action would really change anything? But in the end, the truth prevailed, and some very unlikely things have happened.

The reason I discuss these things is in the context of Jesus in India. I have tried to resist firm conclusions in this book, preferring to point the way with a mixture of evidence, facts, conjecture and reason. But I do have one conclusion I would like you to take with you. I conclude that for two thousand years the truth has been hidden from us, from the masses of ordinary people who have relied upon the New Testament as an accurate historical documentation of true events. We have only been told the parts of the story that a politically structured committee (the Council of Nicea) in 325 A.D. wanted us to hear, and that both embellishments and omissions have been many.

It is my belief that an avalanche is coming. That avalanche will begin in small ways, by people searching for the real truth about the life of Jesus. It will gain momentum as scholars, academicians, researchers and people from all walks of life discover more and more evidence pointing in the same direction. That direction will show that the mysterious, missing years in the life of Jesus was a time of intense travel and study and even of deliberate provocation against some of the entrenched structures of Hinduism in India in his time, such as the caste system and rules affecting the so-called "Untouchables." Jesus supported the "Untouchables" everywhere, and in Judea, as we know, that included sympathy for those with leprosy. The accounts of his actions in India, written by Buddhists, is entirely consistent with what we would expect of the Jesus we think we know. Even without the document of **"The Life of Saint Issa: The Best of the Sons of Men"** in our hands, so we could carbon date the text of the original Pali language version of it, I have found no reasons to reject its probable authenticity, based on the trail of evidence examined in this book and elsewhere. Christians of the future will take more seriously the words of John 21:25, which are the closing words of the four canonical Gospels: "And there are also many other things which Jesus did, the which, if they should be written every one, I suppose that even the world itself could not contain the books that should be written. Amen."

As one who was essentially "dis-fellowshipped" from his religious community for an unrelenting inquiry into valid and legitimate issues, I live for the day that Christians of the future will be more open-minded and more willing to embrace historical evidence without regarding discoveries of history and science and even so-called "paranormal phenomena" as potential threats to entrenched and cherished beliefs, or as the work of the devil.

Yes, an avalanche of new thinking and inquiry is coming.

The avalanche will result in a significant, profound evolution of the spiritual beliefs and thinking of large numbers of ordinary people. As a result, our spiritual outlook and belief systems will be transformed, and I should think (and sincerely hope) that would be a transformation for the better.

Symbolic of the tragedy of violence and a reminder of the consequences of intolerance, the giant statue of Buddha in Bamiyan, Afghanistan, was blown up by the Taliban

13. Bibliography

Abhedananda, Swami. *Journey into Kashmir and Tibet.* Hollywood, California: Vedanta Press, 1987.

Ahmad, Kwaja Nazir. *Jesus in Heaven on Earth*

Ahmad, Hazrat Mirza Ghoulam. *Jesus in India*

Andrugtsang, Gompo Tashi. *Four Rivers, Six Ranges: Reminiscences of the Resistance Movement in Tibet.* Dharamsala, India: Information and Publicity Office of H.H. The Dalai Lama, 1973.

Bedford, Jimmy. *Around the World on a Nickel.* New Delhi, India: Vir Publishing House, 1967.

Bock, Janet. *The Jesus Mystery: Of Lost Years and Unknown Travels.* Van Nuys, California: Aura Books, 1980.

Bruknaer, Nelson T. *The Second Life of Jesus Christ.*

Bushby, Tony. *The Bible Fraud.* The Pacific Blue Group, Inc. Brisbane, Australia (2001)

Cerminara, Dr. Gina. *Many Mansions.*

Coleman, Loren. *Tom Slick and the Search for the Yeti.*

Cronk, Walter. *The Golden Light.* Santa Monica, California: DeVorss & Co., 1964.

Davidson, Art. *Minus 148 degrees: The Winter Ascent of Mt. McKinley.* New York: W.W. Norton & Co. Inc., 1969. [True story of the first winter ascent of Alaska's Mt. McKinley; Ray Genet was one of the climbers and is on the book's cover.]

Deardorff, Dr. James W. *Celestial Teachings.* Tigard, Oregon: Wild Flower Press, 1992.

Deardorff, Dr. James W. *Jesus in India: A Reexamination of Jesus' Asian Traditions in the Light of Evidence Supporting Reincarnation.* San Francisco, CA. International Scholars Publications, 1994.

Deardorff, Dr. James W. *The Problems of New Testament Gospel Origins: A glasnost Approach.* Lewiston, New York: Edwin Mellen Press.

Deardoff, Dr. James W. *A Refutation of False Claims and Distortions by Korff.* Pamphlet. 1996.

Dowling, Levi. *The Aquarian Gospel of Jesus the Christ.* Santa Monica, California: DeVorss & Co., 1907.

Easton, Robert. *Guns, Gold, & Caravans.* Santa Barbara, California: Capra Press, 1978. [The extraordinary life and times of Fred Meyer Schroder, frontiersman and soldier of fortune in old California, Alaska and China.]

Franck, Irene M. and David M. Brownstone. *The Silk Road: A History.* New York: Facts on File Publications, 1986.

Greiner, James, foreword by Bradford Washburn. *Wager with the Wind: The Don Sheldon Story.* New York, 1974, Rand McNally & Co. [Sheldon was one of Alaska's most legendary bush pilots and he had a long association with Mt. McKinley.]

Heuvelmans, Bernard. *On The Track of Unknown Animals.* Cambridge, Massachusetts: MIT Press, 1955.

Holy Bible. King James Version. New York: Zondervan Press.

Hunter, J.A. *Hunter, J.A. Hunter.* New York: Harper & Brothers, 1952. [True story of a professional hunter in old-time East Africa.]

Isherwood, Christopher, trans. *The Bhagavad Gita.* New York: Penguin Books, 1962.

Johnson, Osa. *I Married Adventure.* New York: Garden City Publishing, 1940. [True story of pioneering wildlife photographers Martin and

Osa Johnson who lived many years at Lake Paradise in Marsabit, Kenya.]

Kashmiri, Aziz. *Christ in Kashmir.* Kashmir, India: Roshni Publications, Srinagar, 1973.

Kersten, Holger. *Jesus Lived in India*, 1986, Shaftesbury, Dorset, England: Element Books, 1986.

Kinder, Gary. *Light Years.* New York: Atlantic Monthly Press, 1987.

Kinugawa, Masaaki. *Iai-Do: The Art of Japanese Swordsmanship.* Osaka, Japan: Toyoshigyo Printing Co., 1973.

Kolosimo, Peter. *Not of This World.* Secaucus, New Jersey: University Books, 1971.

Leonardi, Dell. *The Reincarnation of John Wilkes Booth: A Case Study in Hypnotic Regression.* Old Greenwich, Connecticut: Devin-Adair Co., 1975.

Mackal, Roy P. *Searching for Hidden Animals.* Garden City, New York: Doubleday and Co., 1980.

Michaud, Roland and Sabrina. *Afghanistan.* London: Thames and Hudson, 1980. [Absolutely the most dazzling and unforgettable color photographs of Afghanistan are those taken by the Michauds.]

Miyamoto, Musashi. *A Book of Five Rings: The Classic Guide to Strategy.* Kyushu, Japan: 1645. [The true story of Musashi Miyamoto, Japan's most famous and beloved folk hero/samurai.]

Notovitch, Nicolas. *The Unknown Life of Jesus Christ.* London, 1895.

Olsson, Suzanne. *Jesus in Kashmir: The Lost Tomb*, 2007

Pappas, Paul C. *Jesus' Tomb in India: The Debate on His Death and Resurrection*, Berkeley, California: Asian Humanities Press, 1991.

Prophet, Elizabeth Clare. *The Lost Years of Jesus*. Livingston, Montana: Summit University Press, 1984.

Reeves, Richard. *Passage to Peshawar*. New York: Simon & Schuster, 1984.

Roerich, Nicholas, *Altai-Himalaya, A Travel Diary*. 1929.

Roy, Protap Chandra, trans. *The Mahabharata*. Calcutta: 1889.

Sasamori, Junzo. *This is Kendo: The Art of Japanese Fencing*. Rutland, Vermont: Charles E. Tuttle Co., 1964.

Service, Robert. *The Spell of the Yukon*. New York: Dodd, Mead, & Co., 1907. [Classic and charming collection of Service's poems about the Gold Rush and Far North.]

Siemel, Sasha. *Tigrero*. [Adventures of a jaguar hunter in old-time Brazil.]

Rawicz, Slavomir. *The Long Walk: A Gamble for Life*. New York: Harper & Row, 1956. [True story of a 4,000 mile walk from a Siberian prison camp to British India, including the sighting of two Yetis.]

Smith, Warren. *Strange Abominable Snowmen*. New York: Popular Library, 1970.

Snyder, Howard H. *The Hall of the Mountain King*. New York: Charles Scribner's Sons, 1973. [True story of a tragic climb of Mt. McKinley.]

Stevens, Wendelle, ed. *Messages From the Pleiades: The Contact Notes (Volumes 1-4) of Eduard Billy Meier*. Tucson, Arizona: UFO Photo Archives.

Stevens, Wendelle, ed. *UFO Contact From the Pleiades*. Munds Park, Arizona: Genesis III Publishing, 1980.

Thomas, Lowell. *Good Evening Everybody: From Cripple Creek to Samarkand*. New York: Avon Books, 1976.

Valli, Eric and Diane Summers. *Honey Hunters of Nepal.* New York: Harry N. Abrams Inc. Publishers, 1988.

Winters, Randolph. *The Pleiadian Mission: A Time of Awareness.* Rancho Mirage, California:The Pleiades Project, 1994.

Yogananda, Paramahansa. *Autobiography of a Yogi,* Los Angeles, California. Self-Realization Fellowship, 2007

Yogananda, Paramahansa. *The Second Coming of Christ: The Resurrection of the Christ Within You.* (Two Volumes) Los Angeles, California. Self-Realization Fellowship, 2007

Ziegler, Julie H., trans. *The Talmud of Jmmanuel.* Mounds, Oklahoma. Steelmark Publishing (www.steelmarkonline.com)

Bibliography

Author Edward T. Martin at the Golden Temple of the Sikhs in Punjab, India

About the Author and the Motion Picture

About the Author

Edward T. Martin was raised in a small town in the Hill Country of central Texas. During his childhood, on summer vacation trips with his parents, he was able to visit many parts of the United States.

At the age of nineteen, he drove with a friend to Alaska to fight summer forest fires with the Bureau of Land Management. He attended the University of Alaska at Fairbanks, where he later graduated with a Bachelor of Arts degree in Speech Communications. At the age of twenty-one, he made his first overseas trip to Kenya, Tanzania (where he climbed to the summit of Mt. Kilimanjaro) and Uganda. While in Alaska, he was actively involved with parachuting, archery and mountaineering (including a summit climb of Mt. McKinley).

After graduating from UAF, he became a Peace Corps volunteer, teaching English as a Second Language (ESL) in Afghanistan. While in Asia, he traveled extensively in Afghanistan, Pakistan, India and Nepal. During his travels in India, he researched the subject of Jesus in India and found a surprising amount of historical evidence and folklore.

Later, he was a Peace Corps volunteer for two years in the South Pacific, in the Fiji Islands. During that time, he traveled extensively in Fiji, New Zealand and Australia. After leaving Fiji, he lived for one year at Izumo, Japan, where he taught ESL and studied the martial arts of Kendo and Iaido (Fencing and Swordsmanship), earning a Shodan degree in both.

He also taught ESL for one year at Taif, Saudi Arabia, for Siyanco Corporation, and later he taught ESL to Afghan refugees at Peshawar, Pakistan. In the United States he has worked as a teacher, a newspaper reporter and photographer and as the manager of a publishing company. He is an avid student of comparative religion, spirituality, history and foreign cultures. A gifted linguist, he speaks seven languages.

While living in Austin, Texas, he established Jonah Publishing, which published the first edition of ***King of Travelers: Jesus' Lost Years in India***. The two printings of that edition sold out. The book was edited and expanded for the new edition, from Yellow Hat Publishing.

In 2005, Edward T. Martin embarked with Hollywood producer / director / writer Paul Davids on the filming of the feature-length documentary motion picture, **"Jesus in India,"** from Yellow Hat Productions, Inc. The film was three years in the making, involving six weeks of shooting in India at forty locations. Filming took place in a total of four countries (India, England, Italy and the United States) and at six locations in the United States (Los Angeles; Texas; Washington, D.C.; Princeton, New Jersey; New York City and Amherst, Massachusetts). Edward T. Martin appears in the film, which is based upon his research, and he is credited as associate producer.

During post-production on **"Jesus in India,"** the Author moved from Austin to Tucson, Arizona, where he has worked on the TV series **"The Cutting Edge"** (www.ufoshows.com) and has taught English as a second language. In Tucson, he completed writing the book he began in India while the motion picture expedition there was underway: *Jesus in India: King of Wisdom – The Making of the Film & New Findings on Jesus' Lost Years*. That book is also available from Yellow Hat Publishing, a division of Yellow Hat Productions, Inc., which with Paul Davids Productions, Inc., produced the motion picture, **"Jesus in India."**

Mr. Martin is also available for public speaking, conferences, and workshops about Jesus in India and related topics.

Edward T. Martin may be contacted by email at jonahpublishing23@hotmail.com
or at:
info@jesus-in-india-the-movie.com

About the Motion Picture

In 2008, the motion picture, **"Jesus in India,"** was picked up for international television distribution by NBC Universal, which in turn arranged for broadcast of the film on The Sundance Channel, where it was broadcast prime time for Christmas both in 2008 and 2009, as well as showing during Easter and August of 2008. It has been licensed for TV all around the world, including by Showtime in Australia, with other pay TV showings in Brazil, Canada, Portugal, Poland, and many other countries.

The DVD of **"Jesus in India"** is available at www.jesus-in-india-the-movie.com. Orders at the website can be shipped anywhere in the world.

The DVD is a widescreen special edition with the 97 minute feature and an additional 80 minutes of bonus materials. The special features include Edward T. Martin on **"The Cutting Edge"** TV show. There are also in-depth commentaries filmed at the Film Forecast Conference at Big Bear Lake, California in June, 2008. Producer / Director / Editor Paul Davids appeared there with fellow producer-editor Anil Kumar Urmil, along with Assistant Director Nelvan Thomas Binny of Mumbai, India. Composer Brian Thomas Lambert also appeared.

There are also deleted scenes and extended interviews with some of those who appear in the film, as well as photos of the crew in India.

You can learn more about the film's director, Paul Davids, and previous films he has produced and directed, and books he has written, at www.pauldavids.com His film that will follow **"Jesus in India"** is called **"Before We Say Goodbye,"** a drama about an Hispanic-American family based on a stage play by Patricia Crespin and which includes scenes filmed in the Basilica of the Virgin of Guadalupe.

Learn more about **"Jesus in India"** and the journey to India which made it possible in Edward T. Martin's companion book to this book: *Jesus in India: King of Wisdom – The Making of the Film & New Findings on Jesus' Lost Years.*

Renowned critic Pete Hammond of **Hollywood.com** states that "**Jesus in India**' is a fascinating and profound film, a deeply spiritual journey certain to make you think and question in ways you never have before."

www.jesus-in-india-the-movie.com

You will want to read the companion book to this one:
Jesus in India: King of Wisdom – The Making of the Film & New Findings on Jesus' Lost Years:

Printed in the United States of America